▶ KU-181-935

WATERFORD CITY
LIBRARY

2540253	
L B C	128076
	E7.23

Essential China

by Paul Mooney

Paul Mooney has lived in Greater China for
more than two decades as a student and
journalist. He has travelled widely throughout
China, Hong Kong and Taiwan writing
articles on economics, politics, society and
travel. He is also the author of guidebooks
on Taipei and Taiwan. Paul now lives in
Beijing with his wife and two daughters,
where he continues to write about China.

Above: *Pan Men Gate, Suzhou*

AA Publishing

Cultural show, Guizhou

Written by Paul Mooney

Published and distributed in the United Kingdom by AA Publishing, a trading name of Automobile Association Developments Limited, whose registered office is Millstream, Maidenhead Road, Windsor, Berkshire, SL4 5GD.
Registered number 1878835.

© Automobile Association Developments Limited 2003
Maps © CPA Media 2003

Automobile Association Developments Limited retains the copyright in the original edition © 2003 and in all subsequent editions, reprints and amendments.

A CIP catalogue record for this book is available from the British Library.

ISBN 0 7495 3773 6

All rights reserved. No part of this publication may be reproduced, stored in a retrieval system, or transmitted in any form or by any means – electronic, photocopying, recording or otherwise – unless the written permission of the publishers has been obtained beforehand. This book may not be sold, resold, hired out or otherwise disposed of by way of trade in any form of binding or cover other than that in which it is published, without the prior consent of the publisher.

The contents of this publication are believed correct at the time of printing. Nevertheless, AA Publishing accepts no responsibility for any errors, omissions or changes in the details given, nor for the consequences of readers' reliance on this information.This does not affect your statutory rights. Assessments of the attractions and hotels and restaurants are based upon the author's own experience and contain subjective opinions that may not reflect the publisher's opinion or a reader's experience.

We have tried to ensure accuracy, but things do change, so please let us know if you have any comments or corrections.

AO1494

Find out more about AA Publishing and the wide range of services the AA provides by visiting our web site at www.theAA.com

Colour: Douglas Morton, CPA Media, Chiang Mai, Thailand
Printed and bound in Italy by Printer Trento srl

Contents

About this Book

KEY TO SYMBOLS

✚ map reference to the maps found in the What to See section

✉ address or location

☎ telephone number

◷ opening times

🍴 restaurant or café on premises or near by

Ⓜ nearest underground train station

🚌 nearest bus/tram route

🚆 nearest overground train station

🎞 ferry crossings and boat excursions

ℹ tourist information

♿ facilities for visitors with disabilities

✋ admission charge

⟷ other places of interest near by

❓ other practical information

▶ indicates the page where you will find a fuller description

✈ travel by air

Essential China is divided into five sections to cover the most important aspects of your visit to China.

Viewing China pages 5–14
An introduction to China by the author.
China's Ten Essentials
The Shaping of China
Peace and Quiet
China's Famous

Top Ten pages 15–26
The author's choice of the Top Ten places to see in and around China, each with practical information.

What to See pages 27–90
The main attractions of China, each with its own brief introduction and an alphabetical listing of the main sights.
Practical information
Snippets of 'Did you know…' information
Walking Tours
Driving Tours
Special Features

Where To… pages 91–116
Detailed listings of the best places to eat, stay, shop, take the children and be entertained.

Practical Matters pages 117–124
A highly visual section containing essential travel information.

Maps
All map references are to the individual maps found in the What to See section of this guide.
For example, Macau has the reference
✚ 73D1 – indicating the page on which the map is located and the grid square in which the island is to be found. A list of the maps that have been used in this travel guide can be found in the index.

Prices
Where appropriate, an indication of the cost of an establishment is given by £ signs:
£££ denotes higher prices, ££ denotes average prices, while £ denotes lower charges.

Star Ratings
Most of the places described in this book have been given a separate rating:
✪✪✪ Do not miss
✪✪ Highly recommended
✪ Worth seeing

4

Viewing
China

Above: *Nathan Road, Hong Kong*
Right : *Buddhist monk, Linggu Si, Nanjing*

Paul Mooney's China

East v West

Chinese have long debated how to adopt Western ideas and modernisation without diluting their own culture. Confucian reformers in the late 1800s came up with a formula called *ti yong*, balancing Chinese and Western learning. Their aim was to oppose what they saw as the full Westernisation advocated by the reformers and to maintain an essential foundation of Chinese tradition. A similar debate goes on today as the country seeks to modernise, while at the same time preserve its Chinese essence.

The Jinmao Tower dominating Shanghai's Pudong skyline

A story is often told about Arthur Waley (1889–1966), the eminent translator who introduced Chinese literature to Western readers for the first time in the early 1900s. Waley had never been to China, but one day decided he would sail there to see the land he had been so intimately involved with. According to the story, the boat arrives in the harbour, but Waley suddenly has second thoughts. He realises the country will bear no resemblance to the China of his translations and decides not to disembark. He sails back to England a few days later on the same ship having never set foot on Chinese soil, but with his idyllic image of China still intact.

Many visitors to China may share Waley's concern. The China they experience will bear little resemblance to the one seen in movies or read about in books and newspapers. China is a country of sharp contrasts. Walk around an isolated village and you'll see satellite dishes poking from crumbling tiled roofs. Yet nearby farmers manually irrigate fields in much the same way as their grandfathers did, balancing wooden buckets of water on a stick over their shoulders. Yet much of old China is disappearing right before our eyes. Old courtyard houses are making way for skyscrapers and amusement rides are taking over parts of old imperial parks.

As China enters the 21st century, it is grappling with the problem of how to preserve much of its ancient past, while at the same time providing its people with the modernity and comforts they rightly deserve. Time will tell how well the country deals with this dilemma. In the meantime, if you want to experience China's rich heritage, you'd better hurry – the remaining traces of the country's long history are rapidly beginning to fade.

China's Features

Geography

• China covers an area of 9.6 million sq km (3.7 million sq miles). The country is bordered by Russia and Mongolia to the north, North Korea, the Yellow Sea and the East China

Sea to the east, Vietnam, Laos, Myanmar, India, Bhutan and Nepal to the south, and Pakistan, Afghanistan, Tajikistan, Kyrgyzstan and Kazakhstan to the west.

• China is divided into 22 provinces, five autonomous regions and four independent municipalities. Hong Kong, which had been a British colony since the 1800s, was returned to China in 1997, and Macau, settled by the Portuguese in 1557, was made a part of China again in 1999. Both are now special administrative regions (SARs) of China.

Climate

• Because of the size of the country, there are great variations in climate and temperatures, from Siberian conditions during the winter in the far north to semitropical humid weather in the south, and desert conditions in the northwest. The best times to visit are spring (April–June) and autumn (September–November).

• Travellers are advised to wear layers of clothing – thermal underwear and sweaters – in the winter. In the warm climates light and casual clothing is a must. Revealing clothes should be avoided.

People

• China has a population of 1.3 billion people, with 75 per cent living in rural areas. Some 93 per cent are Han people, or ethnic Chinese, with the remaining 7 per cent belonging to one of 55 different ethnic/linguistic groups.

• Most Chinese speak *Putonghua* (Mandarin), the official national language, which is based on the Beijing dialect. Chinese ideographic writing is the same everywhere.

Chinese Names

Chinese surnames traditionally precede the given name and this is the system used in this book. It is customary to address people by their surnames followed by *Xiansheng*, or Mr, or *Xiaojie*, or Ms. For younger people, including tour guides, it is common to precede the surname with the familiar title '*Xiao*', or little, ie Xiao Wang.

Left: *Lugu Lake, Yunnan*
Below: *Chinese vistors at Ming Xiaoling, Nanjing*

Essence of China

Few countries have developed as rapidly as China has over the past two decades. Deng Xiaoping launched economic reforms in 1979, dramatically improving the lives of Chinese in both urban and rural areas. Despite these changes, the essence of the country still lies in its long history and rich heritage, in which the Chinese take immense pride. Wherever you go, history is always there in the background, from the historical dramas that play each evening on the TV, through epic films about emperors, to the cartoons and comics based on fictional characters, such as the Monkey King, enjoyed by school children. More concrete traces can be found in every city and small village: ancient wooden pagodas, magnificent imperial palaces and tombs, serene temples, classic gardens, medieval city walls and beautiful scenery.

Liuhe Ta, 'Six Harmonies Pagoda', Hangzhou

THE **10** ESSENTIALS

If you only have a short time to visit China and want to get under the skin of the country and of the Chinese, here are some essentials:

• **Visit a park early in the morning** for a look at how Chinese start their day. You'll see people doing ballroom and disco dancing, callisthenics, martial arts, sword fighting.

• **Go fly a kite.** Kite flying is a favourite past time among youngsters and senior citizens and takes place in large open spaces, such as Tiananmen Square (► 43) in Beijing

• **Go to a karaoke.** While many Westerners are put off by karaoke singing, it's a national pastime for the Chinese. A good voice is not required.

• **Enjoy Peking duck** at one of Beijing's numerous duck outlets. Spread the thin pancake with some plum sauce, and fill with slices of scallion or cucumber along with crisp pieces of skin and meat.

• **Ride a bike around the city** along with tens of thousands of other Chinese, for whom this is the main form of transportation. Most cities have convenient and safe bicycle lanes.

• **Take a ride in a pedicab.** Take a leisurely tour of the back streets in a pedicab, observing Chinese at work and play, and stopping wherever something catches your interest.

• **See an opera.** Different regions boast their own opera styles, but all feature melodramatic plots, highly stylised acting and magnificent costumes.

• **Take the train.** Rub elbows during an overnight train ride to one of your tourist destinations. Soft berths accommodate four people in a closed room, while hard berths have six people to an open cubicle.

• **Visit a produce market.** Wander around during the early morning hours or just after work as Chinese housewives choose fresh ingredients for the family meal. You'll see a wide variety of fruits, spices vegetables and herbs.

• **Relax in a tea house.** Finish off a busy day with a visit to a traditional tea house, slowly brewing tea in tiny pots.

Huxingting Teahouse, Old Shanghai
Kite flyer, Suzhou Creek, Shanghai

Kite flyer, Suzhou Creek, Shanghai

The Shaping of China

Kublai Khan
Below: *Stone Buddhist stela, Tang Dynasty,* AD. 655

1766–1122 BC
The Shang Dynasty establishes its capital at Anyang.

1122/1027–256 BC
The Zhou Dynasty. Confucius formulates his code of ethics, Sun Zi writes *The Art of War*, and the first Taoist texts are written.

221–206 BC
The Qin Dynasty. Emperor Qinshi unites China and begins construction of the Great Wall.

206 BC–AD 220
The Han Dynasty. Chang'an, present day Xi'an, is established as the capital, and trade routes are developed across the deserts of Central Asia.

220–265
The Three Kingdoms period. Epic struggles between the states of Shu, Wei and Wu.

581–618
The Sui Dynasty. After a period of division peace is restored and a new capital is set up at Luoyang. The Grand Canal is built.

618–907
The Tang Dynasty inaugurates a golden age for music, art, poetry and dance.

907–960
The Five Dynasties. A period of short-lived military dictatorships.

960–1279
The Song Dynasty. Opera developed, literature and landscape painting begin to flourish. Tea becomes popular throughout China.

1279–1368
The Yuan Dynasty. Mongols invade China and establish the Yuan Dynasty. Kublai Khan sets up his capital in Dadu (Beijing); Marco Polo travels to China.

1368–1644
The Ming Dynasty. The Chinese overthrow the Mongols. Jesuit scholars win favour at the Imperial Court.

1644–1911
The Qing Dynasty. Invading Manchus take advantage of an imperial court weakened by corruption to establish the Qing Dynasty.

1839–1842
Chinese authorities seize foreign opium at Canton, leading to the First Opium War the following year.

1842
Treaty of Nanjing ends the war: five treaty ports are opened to foreigners; Hong Kong is ceded to Britain.

1850–1864
Hong Xiuquan, a failed scholar, leads Taiping Rebellion.

1862
Empress Dowager Cixi named regent to the child emperor Tongzhi, starts her 48-year reign as de facto ruler of China.

1897–1898
Germans, British, French, and Russians sign conventions with China, turning large chunks of Chinese territory over to these European powers.

1900
The Boxer Rebellion, an anti-Christian, anti-foreign uprising, racks Beijing.

1908
Emperor Puyi, China's Last Emperor, accedes to the throne.

1911
Revolution breaks out in Wuchang. Sun Yatsen is declared president.

1912
Republic of China established on January 1.

1921
Chinese Communist Party is formed.

1934
Chinese Communists, led by Mao Zedong, begin the Long March.

1937
War breaks out between China and Japan. The Rape of Nanjing (➤ 64)

occurs in December.

1945
Japan surrenders. Taiwan is returned to China.

1946
Civil war between Communists and Nationalists resumes.

1949
Communist forces seize the mainland. Nationalist forces retreat to Taiwan.

1957
Mao launches the Hundred Flowers Movement. By the end of the year more than 300,000 'rightists' are banished to the countryside or jailed.

1958
Mao launches the disastrous Great Leap Forward (a programme of rapid industrialisation), which leads to famine. Communes established.

1966
The Cultural Revolution begins as Mao issues a directive criticising senior party officials.

1976
Premier Zhou Enlai passes away in January. Mao Zedong dies in September.

1989
The government

Giraffe presented to Emperor Yongle, 1414

disperses student demonstrators at Tiananmen Square in Beijing, ending months of protests.

1990
Deng installs Jiang Zemin as his successor; first stock exchange opens in Shanghai.

1997
Hong Kong and the New Territories are returned to China by Britain.

1998
The Communist Party of China celebrates its first half century of rule. Portugal returns Macau to the Chinese.

2000
China joins the World Trade Organisation.

Peace and Quiet

The earliest Chinese practised a primitive form of nature worship, believing in numerous gods and spirits of mountains, rivers and clouds. In Chinese, the expression 'shan he', or 'mountains and rivers', came to represent the country as a whole.

Sacred Mountains

In ancient China mountains were considered especially sacred, and thus special objects of veneration. Emperors ascended mountains to make sacrifices, poets and artists to seek inspiration, and Buddhist monks and Taoist hermits to meditate. China has five sacred Taoist mountains and four sacred Buddhist mountains, which remain popular with pilgrims today. Most of these mountains have stone steps making it relatively easy to climb. Hotels and restaurants are also available for visitors at the top, and some even have cable cars for the weary traveller.

Nature Reserves

While environmental damage and modernisation have seriously depleted China's wildlife, one can still find a wide variety of flora and fauna in the country's nature reserves.

Huanglong Scenic Area, in northwestern Sichuan, has thousands of highland ponds, five waterfalls pouring over karst (limestone) cliffs, four caves filled with stalactites, and beautiful terraced ponds.

Snow-covered Himalayas, Tibet

Jiuzhaigou, in northern Sichuan Province, is made up of a series of diverse ecosystems. The valley boasts strings of clear lakes, beautiful karst formations and magnificent waterfalls. Some 140 animal species make Jiuzhaigou their home along with many other endangered rare plants and animals such as the giant panda.

Qinghai Lake, located in Qinghai Province, in northwest China, is the largest lake in the country and home to many species of fish. Bird Island is a great place to view cormorants, wild geese, sandpipers, cranes and several species of birds unique to China.

Wulingyuan, a 26,400ha scenic resort in Hunan Province, includes Zhangjiajie National Forest Park, Suoxi Gully and Tianzi Mountain. The area is known for 3,000 quartzite pillars and peaks in a wide variety of shapes, and clear lakes and limestone caves. Zhangjiajie, the first national park in China, has mountain springs and subterranean rivers that converge to form streams. Three minority groups, the Bai, Miao and Tujia, all live in Wulingyuan.

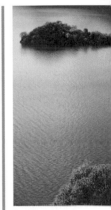

Islet in Lugu Lake, Yunnan

The Humble Administrator's Garden, Suzhou

The Zhalong Nature Reserve is a large wetland located in Heilongjiang, northeastern China. Close to 200 species of bird can be viewed here, including ducks, egrets, harriers, geese, herons, storks and swans. The area is also home to several species of crane, including red-crowned crane and the white-naped crane, both endangered species that breed in the reserve.

Classical Gardens

Wealthy scholars and officials from the Song to the Qing Dynasty, retreating from the world of official life, sought to bring the mountains and rivers to their front doors by building tranquil gardens replicating nature. This made it possible for them to keep contact with their literary and scholarly circles while at the same time enjoying a secluded life. The best of these classical gardens, with romantic names such as Surging Wave Pavilion, Humble Administrator's Garden and Master of the Nets can be seen in Suzhou, Jiangsu province.

13

China's Famous

Mao memorabilia

Mao memorabilia
The Emperor Yongle ,
1403–24

Mao Zedong (1893–1976)

From humble beginnings in a small Hunan town, Mao Zedong rose to become the most powerful man in China. A former schoolteacher with an intense interest in Marxism, Mao oversaw the rise of the Communist party from a small guerrilla-based movement housed in caves in Northwest China to the overthrow of the Nationalists in 1949. Despite the harsh excesses of numerous political campaigns from the 1950s until his death in 1976, Mao remains comparatively unvilified; the official Communist Party line is that he was 70 per cent correct, 30 per cent wrong.

Deng Xiaoping (1904–97)

The son of a Sichuan landlord and a veteran of the Long March, Deng rose to high positions in the Communist Party, falling many times as well. He returned to power after a period of persecution during the Cultural Revolution to take the helm of government in the late 1970s. Following his dictum that 'it doesn't matter whether a cat is black or white as long as it catches mice', Deng launched China on the road of economic reform, improving the living standards of millions of Chinese.

Ming Emperor Yongle (1403–24)

Between 1405 and 1424 Emperor Yongle sent six huge maritime expeditions to explore Southeast Asia, the Indian Ocean, Arabia and East Africa. Led by the eunuch admiral Zhenghe, they are unique in the annals of Chinese history. A seventh and last expedition was sent to East Africa and the Red Sea in 1431 by Yongle's successor, Xuanzong, but after this China turned its back on the sea to become, once again, an inward-looking land empire.

Top Ten

Above: *Old man relaxing in the sun, Suzhou*
Left: *Young girl in festive dress, Guizhou*

1
Bingmayong
(Terracotta Warriors)

28B2

Shaanxi Province, 37km from Xi'an

Daily 8:30–5:30

Buses from Xi'an Railway Station and Xi'an Bus Terminal

Xi'an Station

Xi'an International Airport

Moderate

Xi'an (➤ 49)

Photography is strictly forbidden in the pits and halls

During a drought in 1974, farmers digging a well discovered one of the most amazing archaeological finds in modern history – the terracotta warriors.

The terracotta army – thousands of soldiers, horses and chariots – had remained secretly on duty for some 2,000 years, guarding the nearby mausoleum of Qinshi Huangdi, the first emperor of the Qin Dynasty. The infamous Qinshi, who ruled from 221–206 BC, is best known for his ruthless destruction of books and the slaughter of his enemies.

Each of the terracotta figures – some standing, some on horseback, and some kneeling, bows drawn – is unique, with a different hairstyle and facial expression. Three pits have already been dug at the site in Lintong county, 37km east of Xi'an, capital of Shaanxi Province. Pit No. 1, larger than a football field, is home to about 6,000 life-size terracotta figurines in a large military formation marching east. Pit No. 2 contains hundreds of chariot drivers, horses, cavalrymen and infantrymen. Pit No. 3 is believed to be the army headquarters.

Qinshi's mausoleum lies 1.5km to the east of the terracotta warriors, and it is believed that a larger terracotta army and valuable cultural relics lay buried in the tomb. Hu Hai, the second Qin Emperor, reputedly mandated the sacrificial burial of all the builders and childless imperial maids. Visitors can walk around the site, but it has yet to be excavated due to the construction methods used to build the tomb, which makes it delicate to excavate with current techniques.

Terracotta Warriors, Xi'an

2
Changcheng
(The Great Wall)

One of mankind's greatest achievements, the Great Wall was built between the 5th century BC and the 16th century AD.

The Great Wall was originally built to keep out barbarian invaders from the north and stretches 5,900km from the Bohai Gulf in the Yellow Sea to Jiayuguan in the mountains of Gansu Province. While the bulk of the wall is now in ruins, some sections have been repaired in recent years.

The Ming rulers paid great attention to the care of the wall. As a result, much of the wall in northeast China today dates back to this period. Despite the Ming's dedication, the Manchu tribes who overthrew them poured through an opening in the wall at its eastern terminus in 1644 when the Ming general Wu Sangui defected to the Manchu side, leaving the Shanhai Pass unguarded.

The most accessible sites for tourists are Badaling and Mutianyu. These are also the most commercial and crowded sections of the wall. The best views can be found at Simatai and Jinshanling, a slightly longer drive from the capital, where less restoration work has been carried out, and where fewer tourists venture. There are cable cars at Simatai and Mutianyu for those who have trouble negotiating the steep steps.

✚ 29D3

✉ Badaling, Yanqing county; Jinshanling, Miyun county; Mutianyu, Huairou county; Simatai, Miyun county

☎ Badaling (010) 6912 1235; Mutianyu (010) 6964 2062; Simatai (010) 6993 1095

🍴 Restaurants at entrance points (£–££)

🚌 Badaling: Buses from Qianmen; Beijing Railway Station; Dongdaqiao and Andingmen, most weekends only
Mutianyu: 6 from Xuanwumen or Dongsi Shitiao
Simatai: 12 from Dongsi Shitiao or Xuanwumen

🚆 Badaling: 623 from Beijing Station

✋ Moderate

♿ Few

↔ Ming Tombs (➤ 38),

The Great Wall near Beijing

3
Hong Kong

🕂 73E1

✉ Southern China

🍴 Some of the best
restaurants in the world
(£–£££)

🚇 Mass Transit Railway
(MRT) links all districts

🚌 Bus and tram services

🚃 Kowloon–Canton
Railway (KCT)

⛴ Star Ferry

✈ Chek Lap Kok
International Airport

ℹ Star Ferry Concourse,
Kowloon ☎ (852) 2807
6177

♿ Good

↔ Macau (▶ 75)

❓ Land Between Tour by
the Hong Kong Tourist
Board ☎ (852) 2368
7112

*A colony of Britain from 1841 until it was
returned to China in 1997, Hong Kong is a classic
example of East meets West.*

Hong Kong is a bustling city of contrasts where glistening
skyscrapers dwarf small temples and produce markets.
Cross Victoria Harbour on the Star Ferry for a spectacular

view of the skyline. At
the Star Ferry Terminal
in Central board the free
shuttle bus to the Peak
Tram Station for the
steep vertical ascent to
Victoria Peak. On the
Peak enjoy a bird's eye
view of the harbour and
city below and then take
a stroll along one of the
surrounding paths. The
view is stunning both
day and night. Jump on
a double-decker bus
(get a seat on the upper
deck) for the specta-
cular roller-coaster ride
to Stanley where you
can browse market
stalls or walk along the
beach. Visit one of the
floating seafood restau-
rants in Aberdeen for
fresh seafood. The

scenic 'Land Between Tour' will take you to the area
between the Kowloon Hills and mainland China, a diverse
rural and suburban area where you will visit Tai Mo Shan,
Hong Kong's highest peak, a monastery complex, a fresh
produce market, bird sanctuary, traditional Hakka village
and a fish farm. A 40-minute ferry ride will whisk you from
the booming Central district to one of the many serene
offshore islands where you'll see fishermen tending their
nets and farmers working in the fields. Take a ferry to
Lantau Island to visit the Po Lin Monastery, home of a
huge seated Buddha. Stay for a vegetarian lunch at the
temple and then visit the nearby fishing village of Tai O. Or
take a ride out to Lamma Island and walk along small paths
past old farmhouses and up into the hills for spectacular
sea views. Finish with an inexpensive seafood meal by the
water as the sun goes down.

*The Lippo Towers in
downtown Hong Kong*

4
Lhasa

The spiritual, cultural and political centre of Tibet. All devout Tibetan Buddhists hope to make a pilgrimage to this holy city at least once.

The Potala Palace is the largest and most complete palace complex in Tibet. It was built in the 7th century, but was destroyed by war in the 9th century. The present structure, located on a hill overlooking Lhasa, was built in 1645 by the 5th Dalai Lama. It is divided into two sections, the White and Red Palaces. The White Palace, built in 1653, is where Dalai Lamas administered government affairs. In 1690, eight years after the death of the 5th Dalai Lama, a local regent decided to build a funerary pagoda to house his remains, and work was begun on the Red Palace. This palace, located between the eastern and

western wings of the White Palace, is decorated with a gilded copper roof, and includes chapels, shrines and the tombs of former Dalai Lamas. The inner room of the present Dalai Lama's apartment has been left just as it was on the day he fled to India in 1959, moments before the People's Liberation Army arrived to reinforce Chinese rule over Tibet. Paintings are an important part of the palace, consisting of murals, *thankga*, or Tibetan painted scrolls, and other decorations.

The Jokhang Temple is always crowded with pilgrims and is famous as the home of one of the most precious Buddhist images in China, the Sakyamuni Buddha. The statue was brought here from China by Wen Cheng, a Tang dynasty princess who married the Tibetan King Songsten Gampo. The main hall has a set of murals portraying Princess Wen Cheng's arrival in Tibet.

82C1

Capital of Tibet

The Potala daily 9–1. Jokhang Temple daily mornings only

Restaurants throughout Lhasa (£)

Minibuses cover the city

Flights from Beijing, Chengdu, Chongqing and Xi'an

None

Tibet

All foreign visitors need proper travel documents and a permit to enter Tibet (▶ 81)

The Potala by night, Lhasa

19

5
Lijiang

🕂 72B3

✉ Yunnan Province,
196km from Dali

🍴 Small Chinese and
Western restaurants are
scattered throughout
this small town (£–££)

🚌 No vehicles are allowed
in this old canal city,
which can be easily
covered on foot. Buses
for Lijiang can be taken
from Kunming and Dali

✈ Daily scheduled flights
leave from Kunming and
Jinghong.

♿ None

*Black Dragon Pool and
Jade Dragon Mountain,
Lijiang*

*Nestled beautifully between mountains and
rivers, Lijiang, with its traditional architecture
and ancient canals, is one of the best-preserved old
towns in China.*

Lijiang is one of the few towns in China to survive the
wrecking ball that has transformed much of the rest of the
country. Old wooden houses with tiled roofs face the thick
cobblestone streets, made shiny by years of use. Canals
criss-cross the town, accented here and there by quaint
old stone bridges. At intervals, stone steps descend to the
surface of the water, where Naxi housewives – the
minority people that inhabit the town – wash laundry or
vegetables in the cold clear stream that runs through the
town, much as their ancestors have done for centuries.
Snow-capped Jade Dragon Mountain hangs over the tiled
rooftops, providing a beautiful backdrop to this small town
in Yunnan Province.

Lijiang, one of 23 UNESCO World Heritage Sites in
China, is divided into two parts, an old section and a new
section. The old town, which has not changed much in
recent decades, is the place to visit. The brick and timber
structures are marked by falling eaves and wooden slats
carved with various auspicious symbols, such as fish, a
homonym for 'plenty'. The fronts of the houses are
covered by panelled wooden doors ornately carved with
flowers, birds and other animal motifs. However, the rows
of beautiful old shops have traded their traditional wares

for a wide variety of souvenirs, many of which seem to have nothing to do with the region. Chinese restaurants sell traditional delicacies next to cosy Western coffeehouses serving hamburgers, fries, milk shakes and brownies. Many restaurants place small tables beside the canal, and when the weather is fine this is an excellent place to dine and watch the town go about its business. If you want to beat the tourist crowds, lose yourself in the fascinating alleyways behind the main streets, or plunge into one of the alleys that run up the hills for a panoramic view of its beautiful patchwork of rooftops.

Pictographs from a Naxi manuscript
Below: Naxi musician, Lijiang

The Naxi, a matriarchal people, make their home here, and are easily recognised by their traditional blue outfits and blue caps. Traditionally, property was handed down to the youngest female child, and men tended to gardening and child rearing. The Naxi also have a unique written language, music and dance, which add to the town's rich cultural environment. Elderly local musicians can often be heard performing the ancient music of Lijiang, which is believed to be a form of Taoist music that spread here in the Song Dynasty. The Naxi are known for their shamanist tradition, and unique pictographic script, which is fast disappearing as the older generation passes on. The Naxi have a love for flowers – plum blossoms, camellias and orchids – which can be found in the traditional courtyards.

21

6
Mogao Ku (Mogao Caves)

 83D3

 25km southeast of Dunhuang, Gansu Province

 Daily 8–5

 Buses from Dunhuang. Hotels also arrange transportation.

 Trains on the Lanzhou-Urumqi line stop at Liuyuan, where buses depart for Dunhuang.

 Dunhuang Airport

None

Moderate

Visitors must be accompanied by a tour guide (guide included in the ticket price). Photography is strictly forbidden in the caves. Bring your own torch, or rent one at the entrance.

The Mogao Grottoes of Dunhuang house a rich collection of Buddhist sculptures and frescoes.

Seated Tang Dynasty Buddha, Mogao Caves
Below: *Tang Dynasty ceramic camel with Silk Road merchant*

In the Han dynasty, Dunhuang was an important Buddhist centre because of its position at the junction of the northern and southern tracks of the Silk Road. It was under Tibetan control from 781 to 847, when there was an intense rivalry for control of the trading routes across Central Asia. The caves date from the 4th century, and the site is among the most impressive along the Silk Road. It's said that a Buddhist monk had a vision in which he saw 1,000 Buddhas. He began to carve grottoes into the sandstone cliff, and was later joined by other monks and craftsmen, who over the centuries filled the caves with Buddhist images. There were originally up to 1,000 caves, of which 492 still survive, filled with about 2,400 clay statues and 45,000sq m of mural paintings. Murals dating back to the Northern Wei Dynasty show the strong influence of Central Asian Buddhist traditions. Of special significance is cave 17, which houses a huge collection of paintings, statues, manuscripts and textiles spanning some six centuries. It is one of the several hundred caves that provide invaluable evidence for the history and development of Chinese art.

7
Qingdao

Qingdao still retains charming traces of its brief encounter with Europe.

Qingdao, or Green Island, is one of the most beautiful port cities in China. The city was just a small fishing village until Europeans began to take an interest in it in the mid-19th century. The Russians made it their winter anchorage in 1895, and the Germans turned it into a foreign concession in 1897, using the murder of two Catholic missionaries as a pretext. The Germans gave the city a makeover during their 17-year rule, building Bavarian-style mansions, churches and a train station. Qingdao was then divided into European, Chinese and business districts. The town was given to the Japanese under the Treaty of Versailles in 1919, but was finally returned to China in 1922.

A walk through the streets of the former German Quarter and residential neighbourhoods reveals the city's German heritage. Huaishilou, a castle-like structure, once served as the German governor's residence. The double-spired Catholic church, near Zhongshan Road, and the Protestant church, opposite Xinhao Hill Park, are excellent examples of German architecture, as is the Bavarian-style Xinhao Hill Hotel, which is adjacent to Xinhao Hill Park.

One of the city's most famous institutions is the Tsingtao Brewery (this is the older spelling of the city's name). The brewery was founded in 1903 by the Germans, and continues today to brew its distinct German recipe in the original copper stills.

Qingdao is also known for its six beaches and fresh seafood – a prominent part of Shandong cuisine.

✝ 29E1

✉ Shandong Province

🍴 Street stalls on Zhongshan Lu (£)

🚌 The No. 6 bus covers most of the city's major sites

🚉 Qingdao Railway Station

🛳 Boats to Shanghai and Inchon, South Korea

✈ Qingdao Airport

♿ None

❓ Beer Festival, August

Huaishilou – former Residence of the German governor in Qingdao

23

8
Yangshuo

73D2

83km from Guilin by boat, Guangxi Province

Chinese and Western restaurants on main street (£)

Buses from Guilin, Liuzhou and Guangzho

Guilin Railway Station

Li River Cruise; Wuzhou–Hong Kong High Speed Ferry

Guilin Airport

None

Guilin (➤ 73)

With its amazing karst formations, Yangshuo is like falling into a Chinese landscape painting.

Yangshuo has in recent years become a Mecca for foreign backpackers, lured by the beautiful scenery.

The best way to explore the nearby countryside is by bicycle, passing bamboo groves, orange orchards, cinnamon trees, and fields of sugar cane, peanuts, watermelons and tobacco. Moon Hill, a limestone peak marked by a moon-shaped hole, is a 10km bike ride southwest of Yangshuo. A 30-minute hike to the top provides excellent views of the surrounding countryside.

Boat tours out of Yangshuo travel upriver to Xingping, or downstream to Fuli. Xingping is known for its beautiful natural scenery. In addition to amazing views, Fuli, a small fishing and farming area with traditional architecture, offers charming narrow streets. You can also hire your own small boat (about Rmb200) for a leisurely trip down the Li River, getting off to explore rustic villages that still practise fishing with tamed cormorants.

Karst outcrops rise over the Li River, Yangshuo

Cobblestoned Xi Jie, or West Street, has a wide array of souvenir shops selling a variety of arts and crafts. Diecui Road is a good place for a look at a local produce market. For those in need of a brief break from China, dine outside at one of the local Western restaurants that serve up inexpensive Western dishes. These restaurants and coffee shops are good places to get advice on touring the area.

9
Yangzi Jiang
(Yangtze River)

Rising in the icy mountains of Qinghai Province, the Yangzi passes through seven provinces, ending its journey in the East China Sea.

The Yangzi, at 6,380km in length, is the third longest river in the world, dividing China between the wheat-growing north and the rice-growing south. Every turn brings to mind stories from history and mythology, such as Kublai Khan's crossing of the river on his conquest of the Song dynasty in the 13th century.

Starting at Chongqing and heading down river the first stopping point is Fengdu, with its temples dedicated to the King of the Underworld. Further downstream, Wanxian, an old port city with a lively night market, is where many boats dock for the evening. Baidicheng provides views of the Qutang Gorge, the first of the three gorges.

The Three Gorges, located on a 200km length of the river between Baidicheng and Yichang, are crowded with towering peaks, jagged cliffs and caves. Qutang is the shortest, but most beautiful, of the three. Wu, or Sorceress Gorge, is surrounded by sloping forests and strange mountain peaks. Xiling, the last and longest, is marked by shoals and rapids. At Wushan travellers can disembark for an excursion through the Three Lesser Gorges of the Daning River, riding the crystal clear shallow waters in small boats through scenery that is almost surreal.

At Yichang you can visit the construction site of the Three Gorges Dam, the largest dam project in the world.

Wuhan, made an international Treaty Port during the mid-19th century when China's doors were forced open, is the major inland river port along the Yangzi. This is the stopping point for most river cruises.

🚩 72C3

✉ Central China

🍴 Cruise ships and steamers serve food

🚢 Boats from Chongqing to Wuhan (4 days, 3 nights)

♿ None

❓ Tours can be arranged through the China International Travel Service (CITS) and international travel agencies. Note that a variety of boats can be booked, from simple steamers to expensive cruise ships.

The Upper Yangzi or 'River of Golden Sand'

Socialist statuary on the Yangzi Bridge at Nanjing

25

10
Zijincheng
(Forbidden City)

⊕ 35D3

✉ Xichangan Jie, Beijing

☎ (010) 6513 2255

Established between 1406 and 1420, the Forbidden City remains the most complete collection of imperial architecture in China.

🕐 8:30–5 (Last tickets 3:30)

🍴 Starbucks Coffee at southern entrance (£)

Ⓜ Tiananmen East or Tiananmen West

🚌 1, 2, 4, 10, 20, 52, 57, 101

♿ None

✋ Moderate

↔ Beihai Park (➤ 32), Jingshan Park (➤ 33), Qianmen (➤ 37)

With 9,999 rooms the Imperial Palace (Forbidden City) – the home of China's emperors from 1420 to 1911 – is the largest palace complex in the world. The palace was rebuilt many times, but always retained the original design. The wall that surrounds the complex, anchored at the corners by four guard towers, is in turn encircled by a moat. The palace is divided into three sections: the palace gates, principal halls and inner court.

After passing through the Gate of Heavenly Peace (Tiananmen) and the Upright Gate you reach the Meridian Gate, the traditional entrance to the Forbidden City. Only the emperor was permitted to enter here. Beyond this is the final portal, the Gate of Supreme Harmony.

The outer courtyard was designed to accommodate 90,000 people during ceremonies. In the centre stands the Hall of Supreme Harmony. Important ceremonies were held here, including the emperor's birthday. Behind this stand the Hall of Complete Harmony, where the emperor dressed for functions, and the Hall of Preserving Harmony. Within the inner courtyard the Palace of Heavenly Purity, Hall of Heavenly and Terrestrial Union and Palace of Terrestrial Tranquillity were used for lesser functions. The Palace of Terrestrial Tranquillity was where the emperors consummated their marriages. The smaller courts in the east and west are where the imperial families, concubines and attendants lived. Behind this is the Imperial Garden.

The Forbidden City viewed from Coal Hill, Beijing

What to See

Above: *Golden bodhisattva images at Longhua Temple, Shanghai*
Right: *Miao girl in traditional costume, Guizhou*

27

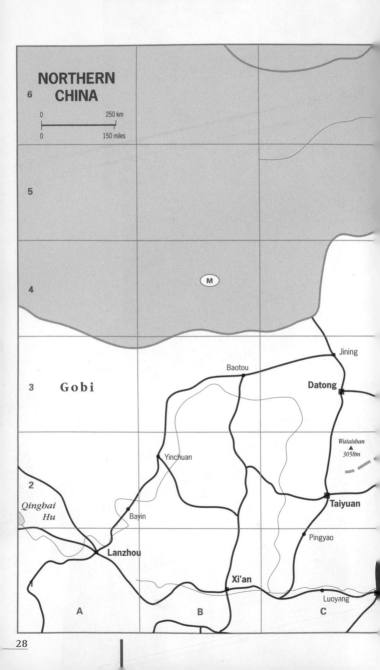

NORTHERN CHINA

6

0   250 km
0   150 miles

5

4   M

3   G o b i

Jining

Baotou

Datong

Wutaishan
▲ *3058m*

Yinchuan

2

Qinghai Hu

Bayin

Taiyuan

Pingyao

Lanzhou

Xi'an

Luoyang

A   B   C

Beijing & Northern China

This region of China covers the northeastern part of the country, with widely different terrains and climates. It includes the special municipalities of Beijing and Tianjin, rapidly expanding modern commercial centres. There is also the industrialised Northeast area, formerly known as Manchuria, the birthplace of the Manchus, with its long and bitter cold winters, but temperate summers. Inner Mongolia, covered by the Gobi Desert in the north and long stretches of grasslands in the south, is known for its scenery and outdoor life. Beijing, with its many historical sites, is the most important area for tourists, and so dominates this region.

' On the banks of a great river in the province of Cathay there stood an ancient city of great size and splendour which was named Khanbaliq, or the Khan's city. '

MARCO POLO
after visiting the Chinese capital in the 13th century

Beijing

It was not until Kublai Khan established the Yuan Dynasty, that Beijing, then called Dadu, or Great Capital, became the capital of all of China for the first time. In 1368, the Chinese changed the name to Beiping, or 'northern peace'. In the Ming Dynasty, Emperor Yongle, known as the architect of Beijing, began a massive rebuilding of the city, including the Temple of Heaven and the Imperial Palace, a project that took 14 years to complete. To protect the city, a massive city wall, complete with looming watchtowers, was erected. After the Manchus overthrew the Ming Dynasty in 1644, they expanded the Forbidden City and built several pleasure palaces on the outskirts.

Beijing remained the imperial capital under the Qing, though the Nationalists set up their capital in Nanjing in the 1920s, where it remained until 1949, when they retreated to Taiwan. The Red Army marched into Beijing in the same year, and once again the city became China's capital. Beijing changed dramatically over the subsequent five decades, with the old city wall being torn down in the 1950s.

The White Dagoba in Beijing's Beihai Park

The city's real boom came after economic reforms were launched in the 1980s. Many infrastructure projects were carried out at the turn of the century as the Communist Party marked its fifth decade in power, and as the government made a successful push to host the 2008 Olympics. Unfortunately, many old lanes or *hutong*, courtyard houses and historical sites have disappeared under the weight of the wrecking ball as new apartment complexes and office buildings rise in their place. The authorities today face the challenge of promoting modernisation without erasing the charm of the old city.

What to See in Beijing

BAIYUNGUAN (WHITE CLOUD TEMPLE) ✪✪

✚ 34B2
✉ 6 Baiyunguan Jie,
   Xibianmenwai, Xuanwu
   District
☎ (010) 6346 3887
🕐 Daily 8:30–4:30
🚇 Fuxingmen
🚌 46, 48, 114, 308
✋ Cheap

This is one of the major Taoist temples in China, and today the headquarters of the China Taoist Association. The first Taoist monastery was erected here in the 8th century, but the present structure underwent major renovations in 1956 and 1981. The monastery conducts traditional ceremonies and is regularly crowded with followers and tourists on holy days. Temple decorations contain many of their religious symbols, including Lingzhi fungus, cranes and storks.

BEIHAI GONGYUAN (BEIHAI PARK) ✪✪

✚ 34C4
✉ Wenjin Jie, Xicheng
   District
☎ (010) 6407 1415

Beihai Park was once the pleasure palace for emperors of the Liao, Jin, Yuan, Ming and Qing dynasties.

The most important structure here is the Hall of Receiving Light, which is home to a 5m-high white jade

Boats in Beihai Park

🕐 Daily 6.30–8 in winter, 9
   in summer
🚌 5, 101, 103, 109, to south
   gate: 13, 42, 105, 107,
   111, 118
✋ Cheap

Buddha said to have been a gift from Burma to the Empress Dowager Cixi. This is where emperors rested when on their way to the western suburbs.

Qionghua Island, in Lake Beihai, is the location of the White Dagoba and the Pavilion of Benevolent Voice, offering excellent views of the surrounding lakes.

FAYUANSI (FAYUAN TEMPLE) ✪✪

✚ 34C1
✉ 7 Fayuansiqian Jie,
   Xuanwu District
☎ (010) 6353 4171
🕐 Thu–Tue 8:30–11, 2–4
🚌 6, 50, 53, 56, 61, 109
♿ None

This temple was built in 654 in the Tang Dynasty to honour soldiers killed in battle. Home of the Buddhist Theoretical Institute, the temple is often crowded with Buddhist monks going to and from classes. The temple houses an excellent collection of artefacts and manuscripts dating from the Ming and Qing dynasties

Young boy at Kong Miao Confucius Temple, Beijing

GUGUANG XIANGTAI (OBSERVATORY) ○○

The Chinese have placed great importance on astronomy since ancient times, with dynasties building observatories in their capitals so that astronomers could produce the official calendar that regulated the agricultural year and sacred ceremonies. Kublai Khan established an observatory just north of here in the Yuan Dynasty. The Ming court built the present observatory at this watchtower in 1442, and it remained in use until 1929. The original Ming and Qing instruments are displayed outside on the second level terrace.

- 35F2
- 2 Dongbiaobei Hutong, Chaoyang District
- (010) 6524 2202
- Wed–Sun 9–11:30, 1–4:30
- Jianguomen
- 1, 4, 8, 9, 20, 43, 44, 57
- Moderate

JINGSHAN GONGYUAN (PROSPECT HILL PARK) ○

Jingshan Park, which dates back to the Yuan Dynasty, was once the private playground of the imperial family. When the moat was dug for the Forbidden City, the excavated earth was used to create five hills north of the Imperial Palace. The Ten Thousand Spring Pavilion at the top of the central peak provides a panoramic view of the gold and russet roofscape of the Forbidden City and Beihai Park.

- 35D4
- Jingshan Park, north of the Forbidden City
- (010) 6404 4071
- Summer 6-8.30, winter 7–8
- 5, 101, 103, 111
- Cheap

KONG MIAO (CONFUCIUS TEMPLE) ○○

Confucius is considered the most important thinker in Chinese history, and his teachings were taken as the orthodox school of thought from the Han to the Qing Dynasty. First built in 1287, the temple underwent a major renovation in 1784. The quiet courtyard is lined by cypress and pine trees, and on the two sides of the yard is a collection of 188 stelae, bearing the names and birthplaces of the successful candidates in the imperial service exams from 1416–1904.

- 35E5
- 13 Guozidian Jie, Dongcheng District
- (010) 8401 1977
- 8:30–5
- Yonghegong
- 2, 13, 18, 44, 104, 108, 116
- Moderate

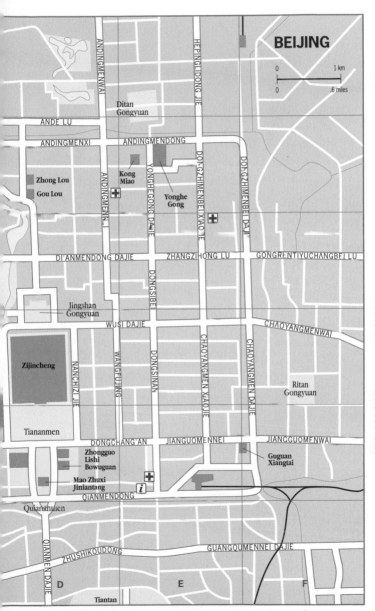

BEIJING

0   1 km

0   .6 miles

ANDINGMENWAI

HEPINGLIDONG JIE

Ditan
Gongyuan

ANDE LU

ANDINGMENXI   ANDINGMENDONG

ANDINGMEN

DONGZHIMENBEIXIAO JIE

DONGZHIMENBEI DAJIE

Zhong Lou

Gou Lou

Kong
Miao

YONGHE GONG DAJIE

Yonghe
Gong

DI'ANMENDONG DAJIE   ZHANGZIHONG LU   GONGRENTIYUCHANGBEI LU

DONGSIBEI

Jingshan
Gongyuan

WUSI DAJIE   CHAOYANGMENWAI

Zijincheng

NANCHIZI JIE

WANGFUJING

DONGSINAN

CHAOYANGMEN XIAOJIE

CHAOYANGMEN DAJIE

Ritan
Gongyuan

Tiananmen

DONGCHANG'AN   JIANGUOMENNEI   JIANGGUOMENWAI

Zhongguo
Lishi
Bowuguan

Mao Zhuxi
Jiniantang

Guguan
Xiangtai

QIANMENDONG

Quianantien

ZHUSHIKOUDONG   GUANGQUMENNEI DAJIE

QIANMEN DAJIE

D   E   F

Tiantan

35

+ 35D2
⊠ Tiananmen Square
☎ (010) 6513 2277
⏰ Mon–Sat 8:30–11:30, Mon, Wed and Fri 2–4
🚇 Tiananmen, Qianmen
🚌 1, 2, 4, 5, 9, 10, 17, 22, 44, 47, 48, 53, 59, 110, 116
✋ Free

MAO ZHUXI JINIANTANG (MAO MEMORIAL HALL) ✪

After Chairman Mao Zedong died in 1976, the party ignored his wish to be cremated and ordered that his body be embalmed. Within one year, the Mao mausoleum was built at the southern end of Tiananmen Square, and his body was placed in a crystal coffin draped with the red flag of the Communist Party. The coffin, located in the Hall of Mourning, is raised from its underground refrigeration unit each morning. A visit here takes just a few minutes as viewers are not permitted to stop.

+ 34C2
⊠ 181 Qianmenxi Jie, Xuanwumendong Dajie, Xuanwu District
☎ (010) 6603 7139
⏰ Services in Latin, Mon–Fri 6AM, Sat 6:30AM. Service in English, Sun 10AM
🚇 Xuanwumen
🚌 5, 15, 25, 44, 45, 48, 49

NANTANG (SOUTHERN CATHEDRAL) ✪

The Southern Cathedral, also known as the Cathedral of the Immaculate Conception, is the oldest Catholic church in Beijing. It was first erected in the middle of the 16th century by Matteo Ricci, an Italian Jesuit missionary who arrived in China in 1583, and received permission to live in Beijing in 1601 after impressing Emperor Wanli with his knowledge of maths and science. The cathedral was rebuilt in 1657, and a stone tablet erected at the time still stands in the yard, inscribed with the words 'Cathedral Built on Imperial Order'. The present structure dates back to 1904.

+ 34B1
⊠ 88 Niu Jie, Xuanwu District
☎ (010) 6353 2564
⏰ Daily 8–4:30
🚌 61
✋ Moderate

NIUJIE LIBAISI (NIUJIE MOSQUE) ✪✪

One of the oldest mosques in Beijing, it was built by the son of an Arab *imam* who came to China in 996, but it has since undergone numerous renovations. Many of the early Muslims who arrived in China during the Yuan Dynasty are buried on the grounds. The original structure was built in an Islamic style; the present building has a distinctive Chinese facade. Immediately inside the gate is a hexagonal building called the Moon-Watching Tower. In front of this are a memorial archway, and then the main prayer hall facing Mecca in the west. In the centre is a minaret from which the faithful are called to prayer five times a day.

Mao Zedong Mausoleum, Tiananmen Square

QIANMEN ✪✪

Entry to the Forbidden City was controlled by a series of nine gates. Qianmen, or Front Gate, was the main point of transit between the northern Tartar district and the southern Chinese district of Beijing. The gate was built during the reign of Yongle in the 15th century. The Jianlou, or Arrow Gate, is just south of Qianmen, and the two gates were originally joined by walls. At every winter solstice the emperor passed through this gate in procession south to pray at the Temple of Heaven. Qianmen Dajie, the street running south of the gate, is a bustling shopping area, with many traditional shops.

✚ 35D1
✉ South side of Mao Memorial Hall
☎ (010) 6525 111
🕐 Tue–Sun 8:30–3:30
🚇 Qianmen
🚌 1, 2, 4, 5, 9, 10, 17, 22, 44, 47, 48, 53, 59, 110, 116
🖐 Moderate

QING DONG LING (EASTERN QING TOMBS) ✪✪

Five emperors, 14 empresses and 136 concubines are buried at the Eastern Qing Tombs, including Kangxi, Qianlong, Xuanfeng, Tongzhi and Empress Dowager Cixi. Emperor Shunzhi chose the site because of its good *fengshui*, or geomancy. The tombs of Qianlong and Cixi are open to the public. The marble vault of Qianlong is the most interesting, with beautifully carved Buddhas. Cixi's tomb is also decorated with imperial motifs such as dragons and phoenixes

✚ 29D3
✉ Just before Changrui, Zunhua County, Hebei Province, 125km from Beijing

QING XI LING (WESTERN QING TOMBS) ✪

The Western Qing Tombs house the remains of four Qing emperors: Yongzheng, Jiaqing, Daoguang and Guangxu along with a number of empresses, princes and concubines. The principal tomb is that of Yongzheng, the first Qing emperor to be buried here.

✚ 29D2
✉ At the foot of Yongning Mountain, Yi County of Hebei Province, 140km southwest of Beijing

Islamic confession of faith in Arabic on a Chinese style ceramic bottle at Niujie Mosque

Stone guardian statue, Ming Tombs, Beijing

✚ 34B6
✉ Changping County, Tianshoushannan Lu
☎ (010) 6076 1423
🕐 8:30–5:30
🚌 Direct bus from Qianmen, Beijing Zoo or Di'anmen
💰 Expensive

SHISHAN LING (MING TOMBS) ❂❂❂

Thirteen of the 16 Ming emperors are buried at the Ming Tombs, along with their wives and secondary wives. Only three tombs are open to the public. Changling, the burial site of the third Ming emperor, Yongle, is the most important. It is said that 16 concubines were buried alive with the emperor, a practice that was abandoned later in the Ming Dynasty. Dingling, the tomb of Emperor Wanli, took six years to complete, and Wanli gave a party in his own funeral chamber to mark its completion. The coffins of the emperor and his two empresses and more than 3,000 artefacts are on display in the tomb and two small museums. The Ming tombs are approached by the Sacred Way, the avenue leading to the tombs which is lined with an honour guard of 12 pairs of statues, each carved from a single stone.

✚ 34B4
✉ Fuchengmennei Dajie, Xicheng District
☎ (010) 6616 0211
🕐 Daily 8.30–5.00
🚌 7, 13, 38, 42, 101, 102, 103
💰 Moderate

SI BAITA (TEMPLE OF THE WHITE DAGOBA) ❂❂

This 50m tall dagoba (pagoda), in the Miaoying Monastery, was built in 1079 during the Liao Dynasty, and was significantly expanded and redecorated by Kublai Khan during the Yuan Dynasty. The dagoba's brilliance is said to be due to the fact that it is painted with an expensive whitewash containing a large amount of pulverised seashells. The temple was rebuilt in the Ming Dynasty, and was once again restored following damage during the Cultural Revolution and an earthquake in 1976.

DID YOU KNOW?

Many of the finest treasures from the Forbidden City were taken to Taiwan by the Nationalists in 1949.

SOONG QINGLING GUJU (SOONG QINGLING'S RESIDENCE) ☉

Soong Qingling (1892–1981) was one of the most prominent women of modern China. Educated at Wesleyan College in Macon, Georgia, she later married Nationalist leader Sun Yatsen. The residence has a large, pleasant garden with small ponds, cypress trees and pavilions. The house displays historical photos and Soong's personal effects; the second floor bedroom and study remain arranged as they were when Soong lived here.

🚩 34C5
✉ 46 Houhaibeiyan, Xicheng District
☎ (010) 6404 4205, (010) 6403 5858
🕐 Tue–Sun 9–4:30
🚌 5
♿ Moderate

TIANANMEN ✪✪✪

Tiananmen Square is one of the largest public squares in the world, covering 100 hectares. A public gathering place during the Ming and Qing dynasties, buildings stood on the two sides of a central path leading to the entrance of the Forbidden City. The square is the political heart of modern China. Beijing university students came here to protest Japanese demands on China in 1919, and it was from the rostrum of the Gate of Heavenly Peace that Chairman Mao announced the establishment of the People's Republic of China in 1949. Red Guards held huge rallies in the square during the Cultural Revolution (1966–1976), and a million people gathered here in 1976 to mourn the passing of Communist leader Zhou Enlai. In 1989, the square was the site of massive anti-government student demonstrations. Just behind the monument is the Mao Mausoleum (► 36) and Qianmen (► 37), or the Front Gate. On the west side of the square is the Great Hall of the People, where the National People's Congress meets. The Museum of the Chinese Revolution and the Museum of Chinese History (► 44) are located in the building on the east side.

🚩 35D2
✉ Centre of Beijing City
🚇 Tiananmen, Qianmen
🚌 2, 4, 5, 9, 10, 17, 22, 44, 47, 48, 53, 59, 110, 116

Mao portrait and slogans at Tiananmen Square

Tour Of Beijing

Distance
3.5km

Time
2–3 hours

Start point
Donghuamen, East Gate,
Forbidden City
35D3

End point
Prince Gong's Mansion
(Gongwangfu)
34C4

Lunch
Kong Yiji Restaurant (££)
34C5
322 Dongsibei Dajie
(010) 6404 0507

Begin at Donghuamen, the east gate of the Forbidden City. Turn left at the gate and follow the red wall of the Forbidden City, stopping to listen to amateur Peking opera singers accompanied by musicians.

Ride to the front yard of the Forbidden City, turn right across the yard, and exit on the opposite side. Continue along the wall until you come to Nanchang Jie, the west side of the palace. Ride north to the corner and then turn right at Jingshanqian Jie, and ride past Jingshan Gongyuan (Prospect Hill) on your left. Turn left at the next corner and head north to Dianmennei Dajie, where you will turn left again. Ride past Qianhai (Front Lake) on your right, and then look for the first alleyway (Qianhaibeiyan) on your right.

Here you'll see tricycles waiting to take visitors on hutong tours (➤ 45). At the next corner turn right for a pleasant

ride down a tree-lined street, continuing on to the shore of Front Lake, where you'll find elderly Chinese sitting beneath willow trees with their grandchildren, playing Chinese chess or doing exercises. Cross the tiny Silver Ingot Bridge that spans a channel in the lake and turn left along Houhaibeiyan, which runs along the east side of Houhai, or the Rear Lake. Go around the lake to the opposite side. After you make the turn, you'll soon come to the Kong Yiji Restaurant inside a circular whitewashed Chinese Gate. The restaurant is named after Lu Xun's short story of the same name, and serves tasty dishes from the story.

Back on your bike, peddle to Liuyin Jie on your right. Head down this street to Gongwangfu, the former palace of Prince Gong, younger brother of the Xianfeng Emperor (1851–1861).

Mobile food vendor, Beijing

Temple of Heaven, Beijing

TIANTAN (TEMPLE OF HEAVEN)　　❂❂❂

The Temple of Heaven is one of the best examples of religious architecture in China. Construction began in 1406 during the reign of Yongle and took 14 years to complete. The complex contains three main buildings where the emperor, as the 'Son of Heaven', went during the winter solstice to offer prayers and sacrifices for a good harvest. The emperor spent the night preceeding the ceremony fasting in the Hall of Abstinence. The Hall of Prayer for Good Harvests stands 39m tall and is supported by 28 wooden pillars topped by three conical roofs, all covered with blue glazed tiles. The last person to use the hall was president Yuan Shikai, of the newly established republic, who had imperial ambitions and who offered imperial sacrifices on the winter solstice in 1914. The Hall of the Imperial Vault of Heaven, located in the centre, stored the ceremonial tablets used in rituals. Echo Wall, a circular brick wall surrounding the Imperial Vault, has the acoustical ability to enable two people standing at opposite points to hear each other whisper. The circular mound of the Altar of Heaven, to the south, is where the emperor offered sacrifices and prayed.

➕ 35D1
✉ Tiantandong Lu, Chongwen District
☎ (010) 6702 8866
🕐 Daily 6–9 for the park, 8–5:30 for the Altar of Heaven
🚌 2, 15, 16, 17, 20, 35, 36, 106, 110, 116
♿ Moderate

WUTASI (FIVE PAGODA TEMPLE)　　❂❂

This Indian-style temple was built in the 15th century during the reign of Yongle (1403–1424). In 1473, a temple with five pagodas was built here, each decorated with detailed Buddhist bas-reliefs. The temple was looted by Anglo-French troops following the Second Opium War in 1860 and again by Western soldiers during the Boxer Rebellion in 1900.

➕ 34A5
✉ 24 Wutasicun, Haidian
☎ (010) 6217 3836
🕐 Daily 9–4
🚇 Xizhimen
🚌 4 5, 105, 107, 111, 114

🚩 34C5
✉ 53 Xinjiekoubei Dajie,
Xicheng District
☎ (010) 6225 2265
🕐 Tue–Sun 9–12, 1–5
Ⓜ Jishuitan
🚌 22, 27, 38, 44, 47
✋ Cheap

XU BEIHONG BOWUGUAN
(XU BEIHONG MUSEUM)   ○○

One of the most famous modern Chinese painters, Xu Beihong (1895–1953) is especially known for his vivid paintings of galloping horses. The museum has seven rooms exhibiting Xu's sketches and paintings, as well as an introduction to his life and work. His painting studio and sitting room are displayed here, with his brushes and paints on a table as if ready for use. An unfinished oil painting stands on an easel, as it did when he died. The museum also includes 1,200 paintings by other famous Chinese painters from throughout history, 10,000 rare books, illustrations and stone rubbings.

🚩 34A1
✉ Yiheyuan, northwest of
Haidian District
☎ (010) 6288 1144
🕐 Daily 6:30–6
🚌 301, 303, 330, 332, 333,
346, 362, 374, 375, 904,
905
✋ Moderate

YIHEYUAN (SUMMER PALACE)   ○○○

This complex of buildings and gardens dates back 800 years when the first emperor of the Jin Dynasty built the Gold Mountain Palace at the site now known as Longevity Hill. Succeeding dynasties expanded the complex. The imperial court would come here in the summer to get away from the heat of Beijing. The palace was damaged by Anglo-French troops in 1860 during the Second Opium War, and was burned down by Western soldiers in retaliation for the Boxer Rebellion in 1900, but it was restored in 1903. The 700m Long Corridor, a long covered wooden walkway that runs across the south shore of the lake, is decorated with auspicious symbols and landscape paintings on the beams. Emperor Guangxu and Empress Dowager Cixi received ministers in the Hall of Benevolent Longevity. The Hall of Jade Ripples is where Cixi put Guangxu under house arrest in 1898 after the young emperor attempted to carry out far-reaching reforms. He remained here until his death in 1908, allegedly poisoned by Cixi, who died one day later. At the west end of the lake is the famous marble boat built by Cixi with money intended for creating a modern Chinese navy.

Seventeen Arch Bridge,
Summer Palace, Beijing

YONGHE GONG (LAMA TEMPLE) ●●

After Qing Emperor Yongzheng ascended the throne in 1723, his former palace, built in 1694, was converted into a Lamaist temple. Lamaism, the popular name for Tibetan Buddhism, was practiced by the Manchu rulers during the Qing Dynasty. During the reign of Qianlong the temple became a centre of learning for the Yellow Hat sect of Tibetan Buddhism, and exercised considerable religious and political influence. At its peak, some 1,500 Tibetan, Mongol and Chinese Lamaists lived here. The temple was shut down during the Cultural Revolution, but was saved from destruction by Zhou Enlai. The temple is a complex of five halls and courtyards.

35E5
12 Yonghegong Dajie, Dongcheng District (near the northeast corner of Second Ring Road)
(010) 6404 3769
Daily 9–4:30
Yonghegong
13, 18, 44, 106, 107, 116
None
Moderate

YUANMINGYUAN (OLD SUMMER PALACE) ●●

This palace, a complex of three large gardens, was built for the Qianlong emperor during the Qing Dynasty. It was seriously damaged by Anglo-French troops in 1860 after the Second Opium War, and again during the Boxer Rebellion in 1900. Little is left of it today except for some broken pillars and masonry lying scattered around. The Garden History Exhibition Hall has drawings and models showing the palace during better days.

34A6
Northwest of Qinghua University
(010) 6254 3673
Daily 7–7
331, 365, 375
Moderate

ZHONG LOU & GU LOU (BELL AND DRUM TOWER) ●●

The Drum Tower was built in 1424 during the Ming Dynasty. During imperial times, 24 drums would announce the night watches. The Bell Tower was erected in 1747. The massive bronze bell was rung every evening until 1924, when the last emperor was forced to leave the Forbidden City. It is said the bell could be heard for a distance of over 20km.

35D5
Second Ring Road, Di'anmen, Dongcheng District
(010) 6401 6609
9–4:30
5, 58, 60, 107
Moderate

Summer Palace

🔲 35D2
✉ Tiananmen Square
☎ (010) 6526 3355 (Chinese Revolution); (010) 6512 8321 (Chinese History)
🕐 Tue–Sun 8:30–3:30
🚇 Tiananmen, Qianmen
🚌 1, 2, 4, 5, 9, 10, 17, 22, 44, 47, 48, 53, 59, 110, 116
✋ Moderate

ZHONGGUOU LISHI BOWUGUAN (MUSEUM OF CHINESE HISTORY) ✪✪

The Museum of Chinese History is located in the building on the east side of Tiananmen Square, displaying Chinese history and art through historical artefacts and works of art.

The Museum of the Chinese Revolution is located in the same building as the Museum of Chinese History. On exhibit are more than 3,300 photos, documents and items from the Opium War in 1840, the 1911 Revolution, the May 4th Movement in 1919, the founding of the Communist Party in 1921, the anti-Japanese War of Resistance, the civil war and the subsequent Communist victory in 1949.

🔲 29D2
✉ Jingxi, Nanfangshan, Zhoukoudian Village, 48 km southwest of Beijing

Enjoying a sunny day at Zhoukodian

ZHOUKOUDIAN ✪

In 1929 the discovery of the first skull of Peking Man was found at this site on Dragon Bone Hill, dating back 300,000–500,000 years. The museum at Zhoukoudian introduces the Zhoukoudian culture, including displays of implements used by Peking Man. The fossils disappeared during World War II and have never been recovered.

ZIJINCHENG (FORBIDDEN CITY) (➤ 26, TOP TEN)

Beijing's *Hutong*

For long-time residents of Beijing, there is probably nothing more emblematic of the city than its idyllic – but quickly disappearing – courtyard houses and winding alleyways, known as *hutong*. These have been around for some seven centuries, dating back to the Yuan Dynasty when Kublai Khan established his capital at Dadu, on the site of present-day Beijing. In fact, the word *hutong* is believed to derive from the Mongolian word *hong tong*, which means water well.

During imperial times, there were no street signs labelling the *hutong* and so their names were passed on orally, some named after national heroes, some for their location, and some for the business typically conducted there, such as Cotton Hutong, Rice Hutong, Tea Leaf Hutong, and Hat Hutong. Other names are descriptive. Little Horn Hutong is named for its shape, as one end is much wider than the other. This is one of the smallest *hutong* in the city, its narrow end just 60 centimetres wide.

Despite the changes taking place around the city, time seems to stand still here. Vendors sell *baozi*, or steamed meat buns on the street, next to horse carts piled high with

Dumpling vendor in a Beijing hutong

watermelons. Peddlers push carts down the street, shouting to announce their presence. Some chant rhymes to advertise their wares, and others make a particular sound that residents immediately associate with a certain product. Small children crowd around a hawker with dozens of small woven baskets no larger than a plum, inside which are crickets.

Courtyard houses also represent an important part of the city's cultural history, as many great writers, such as Lao She, Lu Xun and Mao Dun drew from their experiences living within them. 'Without the *hutong*, modern Chinese literature in China would only have been half as significant', claims one Chinese writer.

45

What to See in Northern China

BINGMAYONG (TERRACOTTA WARRIORS)
(► 16, TOP TEN)

CHANGCHENG (THE GREAT WALL) (► 17, TOP TEN)

CHENGDE ✪✪

In 1703, Emperor Kangxi began the construction of a **Summer Palace** in Chengde, known in Chinese as the 'Mountain Retreat to Escape the Heat'. The palace was used by Qing emperors while on hunting trips or making military inspection tours.

The palace area served as the administrative and residential quarters of the emperors. The Hall of Frugality and Calm, which is built of cedar wood, is where the emperor met with court officials, generals, foreign envoys and the heads of northern tribes. The Hall of Refreshing Mists and Waves was the royal bedroom, but also was the site of famous historical events, such as the signing of unequal treaties with the Europeans in the 19th century.

The Datong Buddha

Twelve temples were built outside the palace walls, eight of them belonging to the Yellow Sect of Buddhism for the purpose of winning the support of Mongolians and Tibetans, followers of this Buddhist sect. The structures thus reflect the architectural styles of this tradition. The Putuozongsheng Temple, the largest and most interesting of the eight, resembles the Potala Palace in Lhasa. The Temple of Sumeru, Happiness and Longevity is a replica of the Tashilhunpo in Shigatse, and has a roof with 'fish-scale' ridges and marvellous dragons. The Puning Temple is a synthesis of Han and Tibetan architectural styles.

DATONG HANGING TEMPLE ✪✪✪

Sitting precariously on the near vertical cliff of Golden Dragon Gorge, The Hanging Temple has hung here for 14 centuries. Constructed by Taoist monks known as 'Feathered Scholars' and renovated numerous times, the six main halls and other rooms are linked by winding corridors, bridges and boardwalks. Known in Chinese as the 'Monastery in Mid-Air', the temple was built in stages on pillars stuck in natural and man-made holes in the face of the cliff.

✚ 29E3
✉ 256km northeast of Beijing
🍴 Restaurants along Shanxiying Jie (£)
🚌 Daily from Beijing and Tianjin
🚆 Express train 7155 or 2251 from Beijing

Summer Palace
✉ Lizhengmen Dajie
🕐 5:30AM–6:30PM
♿ Moderate

✚ 28C3
✉ 75km southeast of Datong
🕐 Daily 9–5
🚌 Bus from Datong to Hunyuan. Minibuses from Hunyuan
♿ Moderate

HARBIN

Harbin, literally 'where the fishing nets dry', dates back to 1097, when it was first settled by ancestors of the Manchu people. It remained a small hunting and fishing village until 1896, when the Russian Czar and the Qing court agreed that Russia would build a railroad linking Dalian, Harbin, and the Trans-Siberian Railroad with Vladivostok. Today the capital of Heilongjiang Province, the city retains many traces of its Russian heritage.

Russian Orthodox churches, with their onion-shaped cupolas and scallop-edged domes, were seriously damaged during the Cultural Revolution, but some have been renovated. St Sofia's Church is a good example of Byzantine architecture. The church, completed in 1907, is now the Municipal Architecture and Art Museum, which houses an excellent exhibition of the architectural history of the city. The main part of the church is laid out in the shape of a crucifix, with the main hall capped by a large green tipped roof.

29F5

Capital of Heilongjiang Province, northeast China

Daily from Beijing

Ice Lantern Festival, 5 Jan–15 Feb

Harbin Airport

St Sofia's Church

88 Toulong Jie, between Zhaolin Jie and Diduan Jie

Daily 8:30–5

13, 16, 23,101, 102, 103, 116

Cheap

Pingyao street scene in the early morning

PINGYAO

Pingyao, Shanxi Province, was settled some 2,700 years ago as a military base, surrounded by walls made of rammed earth. The city was enlarged, and the walls rebuilt in 1370. Pingyao remains one of the best-preserved ancient walled cities in China.

In several locations there are urn-shaped enclosures which were designed to trap invaders. There are 3,000 crenels and 72 small watchtowers, symbolising the 72 main disciples and 3,000 students of Confucius, with taller watchtowers standing at the four corners.

28C1

100km south of Taiyuan, Shanxi Province

Local restaurants near the Tianyuankui Hotel (£)

Daily from Taiyuan

Overnight from Beijing, daily from Taiyuan

✚ 29D2
✉ Tianjin Municipality, 140km southeast of Beijing
🍴 Goubuli (£)
🚌 Express buses from Beijing every half hour
🚆 Daily from Beijing, Nanjing, Qingdao, Shanghai
ℹ Tianjin Tourist Bureau ☎ (022) 2835 4860
✈ Binhai International Airport

Dulesi
✉ Xiguan Jie, western gate district of Jixian
🕐 Daily 9–5
💰 Cheap

Old bronze coins and strings of cash at a Tianjin antique market

TIANJIN ☻☻

Chinese troops established a frontier garrison here in the 13th century and its location on the Grand Canal made it a centre for the transport of grain from the south to Beijing. 'It is thickly populated and trade is very brisk', a Dutch traveller wrote of the seaport city of Tianjin in the 17th century, 'it would be hard to find another town as busy as this in China'.

The city underwent dramatic changes in the mid-1800s as European powers poured into the city. British and French gunboats attacked the Dagu forts in 1858, forcing the city's doors open to international trade. Tianjin was again occupied during the Boxer Uprising in 1900, and by 1915, it had been divided into nine foreign enclaves, with many Western office buildings and residences.

Major sites include Ancient Culture Street, once a fishing village located beside the Hai River, an uneven attempt to re-create a piece of old China of the 19th century. You can purchase porcelain, books, carpets and other handicrafts here, but prices tend to be high so be prepared to bargain.

Located here is the Temple of Lin Mo Niang, built in 1326 and dedicated to the Goddess of the Sea. Today it is a folk museum. Northeast of here is the Notre Dame des Victoires, an old Catholic cathedral. The **Dulesi** was built in the Tang Dynasty and is one of the oldest wooden structures in China. Visitors to Tianjin can visit one of the many carpet factories where carpets are hand-woven.

WUTAISHAN ✪✪✪

Wutaishan, or Five Terrace Mountain, is one of China's four sacred Buddhist mountains. Close to Inner Mongolia, Wutaishan, with its dense forests and snow-capped peaks,

was a popular pilgrimage site for Mongolians devoted to Tibetan Buddhism. The Tang and Ming Dynasties were the most prosperous periods in Wutaishan, when the mountain had no less than 200 monasteries, but just two of the mountain's old monasteries remain today – the Nanshan and the Foguang Monastery, the latter a good example of traditional Tang Dynasty temple architecture. The valley between these five peaks centres on the tiny village of Taihuai, which has dozens of temples dedicated to the Yellow Hat sect of Buddhism. Taihuai is the jumping off point for travellers.

✚ 28C2
✉ Northeast of Taiyuan, Shanxi Province
🍴 Restaurants in Taihuai village (£)
🚌 Minibuses from Datong and Taiyaun. Private minibuses make trips to various temples around Wutaishan.
🚆 Train to Datong or Taiyuan
✋ Moderate

Big Wild Goose Pagoda, Xi'an

XI'AN ✪✪✪

Formerly Chang'an, Xi'an served as the capital of China for 1,100 years, and the treasure trove of artefacts in the area are a reminder of the city's glorious past. At the eastern terminus of the Silk Road, Xi'an at the height of its glory in the Tang Dynasty was once one of the greatest cities in the world, famous for its beautiful temples, grand mosques and magnificent palaces.

Down the road from the Terracotta site is Huaqing Hot Springs, used as an Imperial resort for hundreds of years. The palace includes gardens and elaborate structures dating back to the Qing Dynasty. It is also famous as the place where Generalissimo Chiang Kaishek was kidnapped in 1936. Other popular sites are the Ming Dynasty city wall, the Grand Mosque, dating back to the 14th century, the Bell Tower, where a bronze bell once struck each morning as the city gates were opened, and the Drum Tower, which sounded the evening curfew.

✚ 28B2
✉ Capital of Shaanxi Province
🍴 Laosunjia Restaurant (££)
🚌 Buses to Luoyang
🚆 Daily from Beijing, Chengdu, Guangzhou, Shanghai
ℹ️ CITS office ✉ 48 Chang'anbei Lu ☎ (029) 524 1864
✈️ Xiguan International Airport (40km northwest of city)

Eastern China

Eastern China includes some of the country's most interesting cities, from bustling Shanghai, a showcase of the nation's past and future, to the ancient capitals that were once ports on the Grand Canal, and which have retained some of the oldest Chinese traditions. Here you will find examples of some of the country's most beautiful traditional architecture. The Grand Canal, segments of which date back 2,500 years, has decayed over the centuries, but remains the longest man-made waterway in the world, stretching some 1,610km. This is also the location of two of the country's most scenic mountains – Taishan and Huangshan.

'When you reach the top of Taishan, you find the world becomes smaller.'

CONFUCIUS
after reaching the top of the mountain.

Boats on old canal at Zhouzhuang, near Suzhou

Shanghai

Shanghai is a relatively young city in terms of Chinese history. Prior to the opening of the five treaty ports in 1842, at the time of the Treaty of Nanjing between the Qing and the British, Shanghai was a walled fishing village near the mouth of the Yangzi River. This all changed, however, when British, French and American settlers teamed up with enterprising Chinese merchants to turn Shanghai into a cosmopolitan city and centre of commerce. During the city's heyday, the Park Hotel on Nanjing Road was the tallest building in China, while succesful entrepreneurs and celebrities from around the world – such as the playwright Noel Coward – mixed it up in the restaurants at the Peace Hotel.

The Russian Consulate by Suzhou Creek, Shanghai

Time stood still for three decades following liberation in 1949, as the communist leadership warily viewed the city's decadent past and reputation for freewheeling capitalism. When China opened its doors to the outside world in the late 1970s, Shanghai was a pale shadow of its past self. The Shanghainese, who pride themselves in being the most savvy and enterprising people in China, lost no time in seeking to revive the city's glory. Shanghai underwent a massive transformation, seemingly building overnight gleaming, state-of-the-art skyscrapers and expressways to speed traffic around the city. China's first stock exchange opened here in 1990, and in Pudong, across the Huangpu River from the Bund, a modern economic zone and commercial centre has risen from land that was farm fields a little over a decade ago.

One of China's largest and most densely populated cities, with 13 million people, Shanghai's bustling streets are today packed with life. Crowds rush in all directions, cars vie for space on busy streets, and department stores and shops overflow with a wide variety of goods.

SHANGHAI

0   1 km

0   .6 miles

ZHONGSHANBEI 2 LU

GUANGZHONG LU

DALIANXI LU

Luxun Gongyuan

GONGHEXIN LU

HUTAI LU

ZHONGSHANBEI 1 LU

ZHONGSHANBEI LU

SIPING LU

SICHUANBEI LU

SONG

TIANMU LU

TIANMU LU

HAINING LU

DONGDAMING LU

Yufo Si

JIANGNING LU

Suzhou Jiang

HENGFENG LU

CHENGDU LU

PUDONG

BEIJING LU

Peace Hotel

Park Hotel

NANJING LU

WAITAN

BEIJING LU

XIZANG LU

HENAN LU

Jinmao

NANJING LU

WANHANGDU LU

Shanghai Bowuguan

Dong Feng

YA NAN LU

HUAIHAIZHONG LU

Yu Yuan

NANSHI

Fuxing Gongyuan

FUXINGDONG LU

Sun Zhongshan Guju

LUJIABANG LU

oong Juingling Guju

ZHONGSHANNAN 2 LU

ZHAOJIABANG LU

RUIJIN LU

LIBAN LU

NAN PU

anzhu Jiaotang

ZHONGSHANNAN 2 LU

LUPU

Huangpu Jiang

PUDONGNAN LU

A   B   C

6

5

4

3

2

1

What to See in Shanghai

FAGUO ZUJIE (FRENCH CONCESSION) ☺☺

🚩 53B3
✉ Huaihai Lu Main Street
🚌 911, 42

Following the signing of the Treaty of Nanjing in 1842, areas of Shanghai were turned over to the foreign powers for trading purposes, and came to be known as concessions. The French Concession, in the area around Huaihai Lu and the Jin Jiang Hotel, had its own buses and trams, electricity, judicial system and traffic regulations.

The heart of the old concession was Avenue Joffre, now known as Huaihai Lu, still the city's premier mecca for shopping. The area has reminders of its colourful past. Fuxing Park, laid out in the Parisian style, with wide paths flanked by trees, is one of the loveliest parks in the city.

HUANGPU JIANG (HUANGPU RIVER TOUR) ☺☺

🚩 53C3
✉ 239 Zhongshandong Lu
☎ (021) 6374 4461
🖐 Moderate

The Huangpu River, just 110km long, runs from Lake Tai and empties into the Yangzi River some 28km downstream. In the past, large ships would enter the Yangzi, make the short journey along the deep channel of the Huangpu and unload their cargo at the wharves along the Bund. The goods were then transported by barges along Suzhou Creek and along networks of canals for distribution throughout China.

The Huangpu boat tours leave every afternoon (and in the evening in the summer) from the Bund.

NANJING LU (NANKING ROAD) ☺☺

🚩 53B4
🚌 11, 14, 26
🖐 Free

Shanghai's most famous street, Nanjing Lu, was once known to the Chinese as the Da Malu, or 'Great Horse Road'. Although now rivalled by Huaihai Lu as a shopping centre it is still popular with shoppers. Nanjingdong Lu (Nanjing Road East), the most lively section, begins at the Peace Hotel and passes many shops, some dating from pre-World War II, modern boutiques and large department stores. A large section of the street, from Chengdu Road down almost to the Bund, has been turned into a bustling pedestrian mall lined by department stores, interesting shops and small restaurants. Where Nanjingdong Lu meets Nanjingxi Lu (Nanjing Road West) is the old racecourse grandstand and clock, and the Park Hotel, the tallest building outside the Americas at the time of its construction in 1934.

*Souvenir shops,
Fangbangzhong Lu,
Shanghai Old Town*

NANSHI (SHANGHAI OLD TOWN)   ✪✪✪

Before 1842, Shanghai was a walled town concentrated in the area now known as Nanshi. Unfortunately, the walls were pulled down in 1911. The centre of the town was dominated then by the Huxingting Teahouse, Yu Garden (➤ 61), and the Temple of the City God. This maze of alleyways is an ideal place to experience old Shanghai. Huxingting Tea House, in the centre of the lake, dates from the 18th century. The teahouse is approached via Nine Zig-Zag Bridge, shaped to throw off pursuing spirits. After leaving the teahouse wander among the narrow alleyways.

✚ 53C2–3
✉ Nanshi District, southwest of the Bund

PUDONG   ✪✪✪

Pudong, located across the Huangpu River from the Bund, is Shanghai's new financial and commercial district. The area is linked to Shanghai by a series of bridges and tunnels. Skyscrapers now stand where farmers planted vegetables just a little over a decade ago. The area is home to the 468m Oriental Pearl TV Tower, which provides panoramic views of Shanghai. The stunning **Jinmao Tower**, the tallest building in China, and third tallest in the World, houses the classy Grand Hyatt Hotel, the highest hotel in the world. Pudong is also home to the Shanghai Stock Exchange and top multinational companies.

✚ 53C4

Jinmao Tower
✚ 53C3
✉ Shiji Dadao, Pudong
☎ (021) 5047 5101
🕙 Daily 8–9
🚇 Take line No. 2 and get off at Lujiazui
✋ Expensive

The Huangpu River and the Pudong skyline, Shanghai

The Bund & Nanjing Lu

Distance
4km

Time
2 hours

Start point
The Park Hotel
✚ 53B4

End point
East end of the Bund opposite
the Dong Feng Hotel
✚ 53C3

Lunch
Dragon-Phoenix Restaurant,
Peace Hotel (££)
✚ 53C4
✉ 20 Nanjingdong Lu
☎ (021) 6321 6888

Start your walk at the Park Hotel, roughly where Nanjing Road East meets Nanjing Road West. Turn left out of the hotel onto Nanjing Road, and walk past buildings that date from the concession days, including the old Wing On and Sincere department stores. After about 40 minutes you will come to the Bund, with the Peace Hotel on your left. The Huangpu River is just beyond the Bund.

Of the many families of Sephardic Jews that flourished in pre-war Shanghai, the best known is the Sassoon family. The family fled from intolerant Baghdad in the 18th century to make a new life in Bombay and then proceeded to buy wharf space in Shanghai. Successive generations invested in the port, but it was Victor Sassoon who built the Peace Hotel, a landmark on the Bund. Many skyscrapers have copied its distinctive pyramidal roof design. Today's Peace Hotel dates from 1930, with art-deco ironwork and high ceilings. Victor hoped the Peace Hotel would be the finest in the East. It had the best that the period could offer, and the Horse & Hounds Bar was the most fashionable rendezvous point in the city. Today, the Peace Hotel incorporates the old Palace Hotel from across Nanjing Road.

Exit the Peace Hotel and turn left to the Bund, and turn left again, passing pre–World War II European buildings, including the original headquarters of the former opium traders, Jardine Matheson, and the old British Consulate. At the Waibaidu Bridge cross to the riverside embankment and return along the Bund for a view of the river. Walk south to the end of the Bund, just opposite the Dong Feng Hotel, the old Shanghai Club.

Nanjing Walking Street, Shanghai

SHANGHAI BOWUGUAN (SHANGHAI MUSEUM) ✪✪✪

The impressive Shanghai Museum is without a doubt the best-designed and most modern museum in all of China. Formally opened in 1996 on People's Square, the museum houses some 120,000 cultural relics, displayed to their best advantage by state-of-the art lighting. The three principal exhibits are bronzes and stone sculpture on the ground floor, ceramics on the first floor and paintings on the second floor. Other galleries are devoted to jade, Chinese coins, seals, calligraphy, traditional furniture and the art of China's minority peoples.

✚ 53B3
✉ 201 Renmin Dadao
☎ (021) 6372 3500
🕐 Daily 9–4
Ⓠ Renmin Square
🚌 23, 49
♿ Moderate

SHANGHAI ZUJIE (INTERNATIONAL SETTLEMENT) ✪✪✪

The British were the first to build a concession following the opening of Shanghai as a treaty port in 1842. In 1863 this merged with the American Settlement to form the International Settlement. Many of its old buildings remain. Sichuan Zhonglu, leading north from Nanjing Lu, will take you across Suzhou Creek to pass a large pre-war building with a huge clock, the principal post office of the city. Where Fuzhou Lu (once notorious for its brothels and opium dens) meets Henan Lu was the Municipal Council, the settlement's administrative headquarters. The Metropole Hotel, which boasted the best food in town in the 1930s, still stands at No. 180.

✚ 53B4–C4
🚌 37 along Nanjing Lu, 21 along Beijing Lu

SOONG QINGLING GUJU ✪
(SOONG QINGLING'S RESIDENCE)

Soong Qingling was born in Shanghai in 1893, the daughter of Charlie Soong, a publisher of Bibles and a supporter of Sun Yatsen's revolution against the Qing Dynasty. After being educated in the US Soong worked for Sun as his secretary, later marrying him. After Sun's death, Soong became disillusioned with Chiang Kaishek, the successor to Sun, and threw her support behind the Chinese Communists. After the communist victory, Soong held a number of posts in the government, becoming a symbol for China until her death in 1981.

✚ 53A2
✉ 1843 Huaihaizhong Lu
☎ (021) 6437 6268
🕐 Daily summer 6–8:30, winter 7–8
🚌 911, 42
♿ Cheap

Tang Dynasty stone Buddhist stela, c AD 655, Shanghai Museum

Food & Drink

China has a wide variety of regional cuisines, with each province having its own specialities. The following are the more popular cuisines that can be found around the country.

Dried flowers for infusions, Zhouzhuang Below: Jiaozi dumpling cook, Shanghai Old Town

Beijing

Mild, but hearty. Wheat, rather than rice is the staple and dumplings, breads and noodles feature prominently. The most famous dish is Peking duck. The meat and crisp skin of the duck and sliced spring onions or cucumbers are wrapped in thin crepes of slightly griddled, unleavened dough dabbed with sweet soybean paste. Soup made from the duck bones is also delicious.

Sichuan

Spicy and richly flavoured, this cuisine makes liberal use of hot peppers. Popular specialities include *gongbao chicken* (diced boneless chicken sautéed with chillies), aubergine with garlic, *mapo toufu* (diced bean curd sautéed with ground pork, garlic, spring onions, ginger and lots of chilli peppers). Instead of rice, try *yinzi zhuan*, a roll steamed or deep-fried.

Hunan

Like that of Sichuan, is known for its use of chilli peppers. The home of the late Chairman Mao Zedong, many restaurants specialise in the favourites of Mao's hometown.

Jiangzhe

The highlight of this cuisine (from Jiangsu and Zhejiang, two provinces located on the east coast), is seafood. This style is also known as Shanghai-style cooking.

Cantonese

Cooking from Guangdong Provincein southeast China is sweet and colourful, and representative of a large agricultural area. The Cantonese are known to eat just about every type of animal, and so according to one popular saying, this cuisine includes 'everything with legs except a table, everything in the air except airplanes, and everything under the sea except submarines'. Cantonese food is perhaps most famous for the brunch time and afternoon snacks known as *dim sum*, or *dian xin* in Mandarin. Waitresses wheel carts loaded with varieties of Cantonese delicacies through the restaurant and diners select what they want from the parade of dumplings, sweet pastries and roasted and steamed treats.

Dim Sum, *known in Mandarin as* Dian Xin

Vegetarian

Called *su cai*, vegetarian dishes have long been a part of Chinese cuisine and contrary to popular opinion, it is anything but bland. This cuisine, often prepared to look and taste like real meat and fish, is served at Buddhist temples and restaurants around the country.

Etiquette

Chinese dishes are ordered communally, with guests helping themselves from the collection placed in the centre of the table. It is good manners to take from each dish what can be eaten immediately; do not accumulate a great pile of food on your side plate or in your rice bowl. In many restaurants there is no side plate, and so you are expected to use the rice bowl as the resting place for food taken from the communal dishes. If there is a serving spoon or chopsticks, use them; otherwise it's acceptable to use your chopsticks to take food directly from the communal plate. Watch your Chinese friends and act accordingly. It may be acceptable to sip soup directly from your soup bowl.

DID YOU KNOW?

Many 'Chinese' dishes created by restaurants in other countries, such as 'Lemon Chicken', are unknown to the majority of Chinese.

Hot chestnut seller on the Bund, Shanghai

🕇 53A2
✉ 7 Xiangshan Lu
☎ (021) 6437 2954
🕐 Daily 9:30–11, 2–4:30
Ⓜ Line 1, off at Sanxi Nanlu
🚌 24, 41
✋ Cheap

SUN ZHONGSHAN GUJU ✪
(SUN YATSEN'S RESIDENCE)

Sun moved to this small house, located on what was then known as Rue Molière in the French Concession in 1920 with his young wife Soong Qingling, remaining here until his death in 1925. Considered the Father of the Chinese Republic, Sun Yatsen helped to overthrow the Qing Dynasty in 1911. As the Nationalist Party leader, he struggled against warlord factions to try to unite China, later helped by the Soviet Union and the Chinese Communist Party.

🕇 53A1
✉ 158 Puxi Lu
☎ (021) 6469 0930
🕐 6PM service Sun, 6, 7 and 8AM on weekdays
Ⓜ Xujiahui
🚌 42, 50

XUJIAHUI TIANZHU JIAOTANG ✪
(ST IGNATIUS CATHEDRAL)

Xu Guangqi, a native of Xujiahui, or Xu Family Village, and an official of the Imperial Library, was an early convert to Catholicism. Baptised Paul, he later donated family land to Jesuit missionaries from Europe for the construction of an observatory and a cathedral. Following a period of anti-Catholic persecution, the church was turned into a temple dedicated to the God of War. After the Treaty of Nanjing (1842) the land was turned over to the French, and two years later a Jesuit settlement was firmly established here. The present structure, St Ignatius Cathedral, was built in 1906 with two 50m-tall spires and a capacity for 2,500 faithful. The interior includes traces of Buddhist symbolism: melons on the nave columns and stylised bats on the windows.

Severely damaged during the Cultural Revolution, the cathedral has been restored and is now a functioning church again, with mass held daily.

Statue of Sun Yatsen,
Sun Yatsen Memorial
Residence, Shanghai
Below: *Yu Garden,*
Shanghai Old Town

YU YUAN (YU GARDEN) ✪✪

Yu Garden was created in the mid 16th century by Pan Yunduan as an act of filial affection for his father. Pan, a Shanghai native who had been in public service in Sichuan Province, must have been a wealthy figure in the city, for the garden takes up almost 5ha, a large chunk of the Old Town. Following the death of the elder Pan in 1577, the garden fell into neglect. It was used twice as a military headquarters in the 19th century, first by Lieutenant General Gough of the British Land Force in 1842, and in the 1850s by the Small Sword Society, an offshoot of the secret Heaven and Earth Society.

The garden is a fine example of a classic Ming garden,

🚩 53C3
✉ 132 Anren Jie, Old Town
🕐 Daily 8:30–4:30
🚌 11, 126
💰 Expensive

with rock gardens, bridges and ponds surrounding pavilions and corridors to create an illusion of a natural landscape. An unusual feature is the sculpted dragon that curls around the top of the garden wall.

Yufosi – the 'Jade Buddha Temple' – Shanghai

YUFOSI (JADE BUDDHA TEMPLE) ✪✪

The saffron-walled Jade Buddha Temple was built in the late 19th century by a monk from Putuoshan to house two jade Buddha figures brought here from Burma. Although the temple has no particular architectural merit, it is a good example of southern Chinese temple architecture, especially the roof of the main hall with its steeply arched eaves and decorative figurines. The highlights of the temple are the two jade Buddhas, each said to be carved from a single piece of milky white jade

🚩 53A4
✉ 201 Renmin Dadao
☎ (021) 6372 3500
🕐 Daily 9–4
Ⓡ Renmin Square
🚌 23, 49
💰 Moderate

What to See in Eastern China

HANGZHOU ✪✪✪

63C3
Capital of Zhejiang Province, 130km southwest of Shanghai
Louwailou (££)
Express buses to Nanjing, Shanghai
Daily from Shanghai (throughout the day), Beijing, Guangzhou, Hong Kong
CITS office ✉ 1 Beishan Lu ☎ (0571) 515 2888
Hangzhou Airport (15km from city centre)

Hangzhou, an old imperial capital, is renowned for its serene beauty. Marco Polo, who visited here in the 13th century, called it the most beautiful and prosperous city in the world. According to a popular saying, 'In Heaven there is paradise, on earth there are Hangzhou and Suzhou'. Many artists flocked here, transforming it into a cultural centre. Two of China's most famous poets, Tang poet Bai Juyi and Song poet Su Dongpo, served as mayors. Hangzhou continued to prosper during the Ming and Qing eras due to the thriving silk industry and location in a fertile rice-growing region. The city was attacked by pirates in the 16th century, and was damaged during the Taiping Rebellion in the 19th century.

The main tourist attraction is West Lake, which is rimmed by small green hills where Longjing tea and mulberry trees are cultivated. A boat can be taken from the northern shore to the man-made Island of Little Oceans in the centre of the lake. The island was designed with four enclosed lakes within the island. Su Causeway, named after Su Dongpo, is a good place to enjoy the lake's scenery. The Tomb and Temple of Yue Fei, a Song Dynasty general and patriot who was unjustly executed, lies on the northern shore of lake. Nearby is the Baochu Pagoda, constructed in the 10th century, but rebuilt in 1933.

HUANGSHAN (YELLOW MOUNTAIN) ✪✪

63B3
1 hour 30 minutes drive from Tunxi
Expensive

Hangzhou's West Lake from Leifeng Pagoda

Located in southern Anhui Province, Huangshan is considered one of China's most scenic mountain areas. According to legend, Emperor Minghuang of the Tang Dynasty believed the Yellow Emperor made immortality pills on the mountain, then called Yishan. The name was thus changed to its present one, Huangshan, or Yellow Mountain. The mountain's rising craggy peaks inspired a genre of landscape painting.

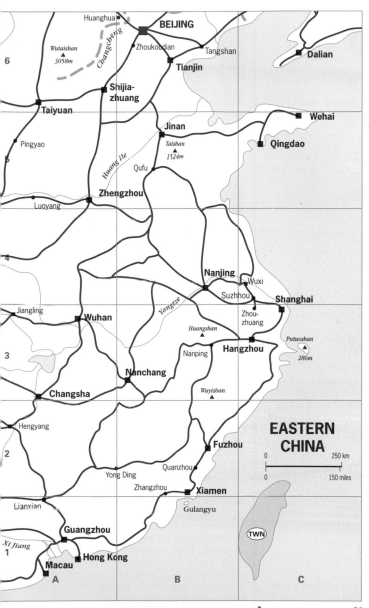

Huanghua

BEIJING

Wutaishan 3058m

6

Zhoukoudian

Tangshan

Changcheng

Tianjin

Dalian

Shijia-zhuang

Taiyuan

Wehai

Pingyao

Jinan

Taishan 1524m

Qingdao

5

Huang He

Qufu

Zhengzhou

Luoyang

4

Nanjing

Wuxi

Suzhou

Shanghai

Jiangling

Wuhan

Yangtze

Zhou-zhuang

Huangshan

Putuoshan 286m

Hangzhou

3

Nanping

Nanchang

Wuyishan

Changsha

Hengyang

EASTERN CHINA

0   250 km

0   150 miles

2

Fuzhou

Quanzhou

Yong Ding

Zhangzhou

Xiamen

Gulangyu

Lianxian

(TWN)

Guangzhou

Xi Jiang

1

Hong Kong

Macau

A

B

C

⊕ 63A5
✉ 90km west of
Zhengzhou, Henan
Province
🍴 One of a Kind Restaurant
(£)
🚌 Buses to Beijing, Kaifeng,
Zhengzhou
🚆 Daily from Beijing,
Shanghai, Xi'an,
Zhengzhou
✈ Luoyang Airport (12km
north of the city)

The bastions of Zhonghua Gate, Nanjing

⊕ 63B4
✉ Capital of Jiangsu
Province, 300km
northwest of Shanghai
🍴 Spring Garden at the
Dingshan (££)
🚌 Express buses to
Hangzhou, Shanghai,
Suzhou
🚆 Daily from Beijing,
Hangzhou, Shanghai,
Wuxi
ℹ CITS office ✉ 202–1
Zhongshanbei Lu
☎ (025) 342 8999
✈ Nanjing Airport (1 hour
south of city centre)

The multiple bastions of Zhonghua Gate, Nanjing

LUOYANG ✪✪

Luoyang served as the capital and cultural centre for 10 Dynasties, covering a period of more than 1,000 years beginning with the Zhou Dynasty. The city was destroyed by wars, but was rebuilt many times. Luoyang expanded rapidly during the Han Dynasty, propelled by the invention of paper and the introduction of Buddhism from India, which led to some 1,300 temples being built in the city. Luoyang also boasted an impressive imperial university and library, which attracted tens of thousands of scholars.

NANJING (NANKING) ✪✪

One of China's four ancient capital cities, Nanjing was once known as 'a home of emperors and kings'. Strategically located on the southern bank of the Yangzi River, it was once the capital during the Three Kingdoms period, the Song, Liang and Tang Dynasties. It served briefly as the capital during the Ming Dynasty, but the capital was later moved to Beijing. The rebel Taiping Heavenly Kingdom made the city its capital for 11 years in the Qing Dynasty, and Chiang Kaishek moved the Nationalist capital here in 1928. Japanese troops invaded the city in 1937, committing one of the worst slaughters in the world, known as the Rape of Nanjing, which left an estimated 300,000 Chinese dead. When the Communists came to power in 1949, the capital was once again moved back to Beijing.

Most of the Ming City Wall (at 42km in length, the longest in China) still stands, including the impressive Heping and Zhonghua gates. The double-decker Nanjing River Bridge, which crosses the Yangzi River, is a remarkable engineering feat. In the centre of the city is the Drum Tower, built in 1382, and the Bell Tower, which houses a huge bronze bell cast in 1388.

PUTUOSHAN ✪✪

Putuoshan, one of the four sacred mountains of Buddhism, is a hilly island about 6km long and 5km wide, with its highest point 286m tall Buddha's Peak. The island is known for its beautiful views and temples, immortalised by Chinese artists. There are two main temples in the north and south. The Front Temple (Qian Si) in the south was built in the 16th century, and was later enlarged in the 17th century. The Rear Temple (Hou Si) in the north is smaller, but more interesting as it is built on a series of terraces on the slope of Buddha's Peak. A large lacquered wood, gold covered sculpture of Guanyin, the Goddess of Mercy, is in the Ninth Dragon Hall. In addition to this, there are 100 smaller Buddhist and Taoist shrines, hermitages and scenic spots.

✚ 63C3
✉ Zhejiang Province, East China Sea
🍴 Baihua Teahouse (£)
✋ Moderate
🚢 Regular boats from Ningpo, daily night boat from Shanghai

QINGDAO (► 23, TOP TEN)

QUFU ✪✪

The birthplace of Confucius (551–479 BC), Qufu was the capital of the state of Lu at the time of the Master's birth. After the death of Confucius, Emperor Han Wudi built a temple to honour the Master. Today, about 100,000 of the city's more than 500,000 residents claim the Kong (Confucius' surname was Kong) family name. Imperial allowances stopped in 1911 when the Qing Dynasty was overthrown, and most of the Kong family fled the city when the Communists came to power in 1949. The adjacent **Kong Family Mansion** is where family members lived until 1937. The mansion was first built in 1068, but the present structures were built in the Ming and Qing Dynasties. The Apricot Altar is the site where Confucius taught his students. The Confucius Cemetery, north of Qufu, is the site of some 100,000 Kong tombs, with Confucius buried in the centre. His son, Kong Li, is buried to the east, and his grandson to the south.

✚ 63B5
✉ Shandong Province
🍴 Seafood stalls on Wumaci Jie (£)
🚌 Regular minibuses to Yanzhou 16km to the west
🚉 Nearest station is Yanzhou
❓ The Confucius Cultural Festival, 26 Sep–10 Oct

Confucius Temple and Confucius (Kong Family) Mansion
☎ (0537) 449 4810
✋ Expensive

A statue of Confucius, Qufu's most illustrious resident

63C4

✉ 70km west of Shanghai, Jiangsu Province

🍴 Songhelou (£)

🚌 Express buses to Hangzhou, Nanjing, Shanghai, Wuxi, Zhouzhuang

🚆 Regular trains throughout the day from Shanghai, also Beijing daily

ℹ Tourist information
☎ (0512) 6522 3131

SUZHOU ❂❂❂

Called the Venice of the East, Suzhou is a city of canals, arched bridges, whitewashed houses and ornamental gardens. It has a history of 2,500 years, but did not prosper until the construction of the Grand Canal during the Sui Dynasty (581–618). By the 12th century, Suzhou became a noted producer of silk. It has long been known as a centre for artists, scholars, merchants, financiers and high-ranking government officials who built fine gardens around their villas where they could enjoy a peaceful retirement. The city was damaged when Taiping soldiers occupied it from 1860 to 1863, but it was rebuilt.

The gardens were designed as small replicas of the natural world, with ponds and hills representing famous lakes and mountains. They also included villas, courtyards, covered walkways, terraces, pavilions and towers, surrounded by secluding walls.

The Garden of the Master of the Nets, Suzhou

63B5

✉ 64km north of Qufu, Shandong Province

🚌 Minibuses from Qufu

💰 Expensive

❓ Tours to Taishan can be arranged by travel agents in Qufu

TAISHAN ❂❂

Taishan is one of the five sacred Taoist mountains in China. Revered for more than 2,500 years, 72 emperors performed rituals here. Since Taishan is the farthest east of the sacred mountains, the Chinese believed that the sun began its daily trip westward from here.

The climb to the top includes 7,000 stone steps leading to the 1,560m summit. Over the centuries, more than 250 Taoist and Buddhist temples and monuments were built here. Climbers need appropriate clothing and comfortable shoes, and those going to see the sunrise or sunset should bring a torch. Due to weather conditions, autumn is the best time to view the sunrise from Taishan. A cable car takes visitors to the top of the mountain.

Bridges and boats at Zhouzhuang

WUXI ✪✪

Wuxi is one of the oldest cities in the Yangzi River delta. When the Grand Canal was dug it pierced the city, which became a distribution centre for grain moving from the rich Yangzi valley to the north. Although the Grand Canal later declined, the building of the railroad in the 20th century enabled Wuxi to remain a trading centre, and it prospered as the silk industry took off.

Wuxi has little of interest for tourists, but Taihu Lake, about 7km away, is popular. The shores of the lake are lined with orange, peach and plum trees. Visitors can take a tour on one of the boats that ply the lake. A trip along the canal can range from a few hours to several days.

Also of interest is the nearby town of Yixing, 60km away, which is famous for its teapots and tea. You can see traditional teapots being made at the Purple Sand Pottery Factory. To see antique Yixing teapots, stop by the Pottery Museum.

✚ 63C4
✉ 120km northwest of Shanghai, Jiangsu Province
🍴 Jinxi Revolving Restaurant (££)
🚌 Buses to Nanjing, Shanghai, Suzhou
🚆 Regular trains throughout the day from Shanghai, also Beijing daily
🚢 Overnight boats to Hangzhou

ZHOUZHUANG ✪✪✪

The old town of Zhouzhuang, with quaint traditional houses standing over arched bridges and canals, lies 30km southwest of Suzhou. The town dates back to 1086 when a noted Buddhist, Zhou Digong, donated 13ha of land to the Full Fortune Temple, which later took the name of Zhouzhuang. Some 60 percent of the houses here date back to the Ming and Qing Dynasties. For a tour of the picturesque city, explore the small alleyways or take a ride in one of the boats that negotiates the narrow canals.

✚ 63C3
✉ 35km south of Suzhou, Jiangsu Province
🍴 Dumpling vendors around the old town (£)
🚌 Regular buses from Suzhou, tourist bus from south entrance of Shanghai Stadium
✋ Expensive

Southern China

Southern China offers visitors a diversity hard to find elsewhere in the country. The area is home to many of the 56 minorities of China, such as the Dai, Bai, and Zhuang people, their cultures rich with colourful histories, legends, costumes, festivals, and their own unique languages. The scenery of this tropical area, known for its heavy summer rains, is startlingly beautiful and varied. In southern China experience the stunning karst peaks of Guilin, the tropical rain forests of Yunnan, Buddhist temples standing beside colonial architecture in Guangzhou, and the traditional red-brick houses outlined against emerald green rice paddies in Fujian Province. Or move across the border to visit bustling Hong Kong, a British colony until its return to China in 1997, or the former Portuguese enclave of Macau, a unique blend of East and West.

*'The Southern Country
has neither frost nor snow;
year in and out you see the
florescence of nature'*

Sung Chih-wen, Tang Poet
c AD 700

Masked dancers of the Miao minority, Guizhou

Guangzhou (Canton)

With its long coastline, Guangdong Province has served as the door for foreigners seeking to penetrate China for more than 1,000 years. Guangzhou, the sprawling provincial capital, today retains traces of its multicultural past in its mix of colonial and traditional Chinese architecture.

Man in temple hung with incense coils, Guangzhou

Indian and Roman traders sailed up the Pearl River to buy silk, porcelain, tea and spices in the 2nd century. They were followed during the Tang Dynasty by Arab, Jewish, Christian and Zoroastrian merchants, and in turn, in the 15th century by European traders and missionaries. In the 18th century, the Canton system limited Western traders to conducting trade in this city under the watchful eye of Chinese merchants. Canton was also the jumping off point for the hundreds of thousands of Chinese who sailed for Southeast Asia and other points in the 19th century. The Qing attempted to put an end to Britain's lucrative opium trade in 1839, when Commissioner Lin Zexu destroyed opium captured from Western traders. The British quickly routed China in the Opium War, which resulted in the signing of the Treaty of Nanjing, and in turn the abolition of the Canton system, and the opening of Canton and four other cities as treaty ports for foreign trade.

The city played a key role in the modern revolutionary history of China. The Christian-influenced Taiping Rebellion, which almost succeeded in overthrowing the Qing, was launched here in 1850 by a man claiming to be God's Chinese son, and Sun Yatsen, who was born in a nearby city, used Canton as a base for a number of uprisings.

Hui Muslim reading Qur'an, Guangzhou

What to See in Guangzhou

GUANGXIAOSI ✪
(BRIGHT FILIAL PIETY TEMPLE)

This Zen, or Chan, Buddhist temple, is the oldest in Guangzhou, dating back to the Tang Dynasty. It was originally the home of a high-ranking official during the Three Kingdoms period, but was turned into a temple following his death. The temple is of special interest because Hui Neng, the Sixth Patriarch of Zen Buddhism, served as a novice monk here in the 600s. The temple has undergone numerous renovations, and most of the present structures date back to 1832, the time of the last major work. The Great Hall, with its impressive pillars, is still architecturally interesting. There are two pagodas behind the hall: the stone Jingfa Pagoda built in 676 on top of a hair of Huineng, and the Song Dynasty Eastern Iron Pagoda, made of gilt iron.

- ✚ 73D1
- ✉ Guangxiao Lu
- 🕐 Daily 9–4
- 🚌 56
- 🖐 Cheap

HUAISHENGSI (HUAISHENG MOSQUE) ✪

The Huaisheng Mosque, one of the oldest Muslim places of worship in China, was built in 627 for Arab traders. The mosque has a stone minaret, the Guangta, which can be climbed for a look at the city. The original buildings were destroyed in a fire in the 14th century, and the present structures date back to the Qing Dynasty.

- ✚ 73D1
- ✉ 56 Guangta Lu
- 🕐 Daily 9–4:30
- 🖐 Cheap

LIURONGSI HUATA ✪
(SIX BANYAN TREES TEMPLE)

This temple also has a connection to the Zen Monk Hui Neng. The name of the temple comes from a poem written by Song poet Su Dongpo, who visited the temple in 1100, and was moved by the beauty of the trees in the courtyard, which have long since disappeared. Su wrote a two-character inscription – six banyans – which is now engraved on a stela near the entrance to the temple. The nine-storey octagonal Huata, or Flower Pagoda, was built in the 11th century.

- ✚ 73D1
- ✉ Liurong Lu
- 🕐 Daily 9–5
- 🖐 Cheap

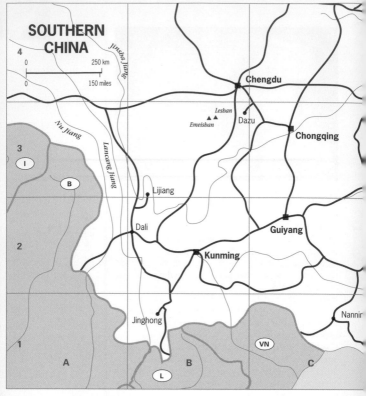

What to See in Southern China

✠ 72B2
✉ 300km west of Kunming, Yunnan Province
🍴 Restaurants along Boai Lu and Huguo Lu
🚌 Buses from Xiaguan, Lijiang and Kunming
✈ Xiaguan Airport (45 minutes from Dali)

The Three Pagodas
✉ 2km northwest of Dali
✋ Moderate

DALI ✪✪

The old walled town of Dali sits on the edge of Erhai Lake, with the Azure (Cangshan) Mountains a beautiful backdrop. The main ethnic group is the Bai, believed to have built settlements here 3,000 years ago, and still known for their colourful dress and beautiful embroidery. The Bai defeated Tang troops in the 8th century to establish the Nanzhao Kingdom, which at the peak of its power conquered parts of Burma and Laos. Nanzhao, later renamed Dali, remained independent until 1253, when it was conquered by the Mongols led by Kublai Khan, who made it part of his growing empire.

The main street, Huguo Lu, is lined with restaurants and shops selling embroidery, batiks, and marble. **The Three Pagodas**, northwest of the city, were built during the Tang Dynasty. The restored Chongsheng Temple, behind the three pagodas, is a good example of traditional Yunnan temple architecture.

GUILIN ⭘⭘

For centuries, Chinese artists and poets celebrated the beautiful limestone karst scenery of Guilin. The area was first settled in the neolithic period, and in the Tang Dynasty it became a centre of classical scholarship, luring artists and poets from around China. The focal point of a visit here is a boat ride down the **Li River** viewing the hundreds of strangely shaped mountains that rise from the plains surrounding the city. The Tang Dynasty poet Han Yu described the river as 'a belt of fine green silk', and the mountains as 'kingfisher jade hairpins'.

Many of Guilin's karst peaks contain fabulous caves with magnificent stalagmites and stalactites. Bicycle or bus can easily reach most of these peaks and caves. It is possible to take a trip with a fisherman using cormorants to catch fish. The trained birds – which have a leash made of wire tied around their necks to keep them from swallowing their catch – dive for fish and then deposit their catch on the bamboo raft.The main ethnic group here is the Zhuang.

✚ 73D2
✉ 590km northwest of Guangzhou, Guangxi Province
🍴 Restaurants along Linjiang Lu
🚌 Buses from Yangshuo, Nanning
🚉 Guilin Train Station
✈ Guilin International Airport

Li River Cruise
🕒 Daily
💰 Expensive

73

72C2
Guizhou Province (east of Yunnan Province)
Local buses to local minority villages
Daily from Beijing, Chengdu, Chongqing, Guangzhou, Kunming
CITS office 20 Yan'anzhong Lu, Guiyang (0851) 582 5873
Longdong Airport (7km east of Guiyang)

GUIZHOU ○○

The backwater province of Guizhou, in southwest China, remains relatively untouched by commercial tourism. Home to the Miao and several other minorities, Guizhou offers beautiful landscapes, with limestone karst hills, terraced rice fields, and rustic minority villages. Guizhou is also known for its colourful minority festivals that take place throughout the year. Use Guiyang, the provincial capital, as a jumping off point for visits to nearby villages. In Jichang village you will see women dressed in Ming Dynasty costumes and many Ming-style houses. Hike through Damochong Valley, known for it rustic villages and

Miao girls from Guizhou

bamboo groves. Or visit Leishan county, the centre of Miao culture in Southeast Guizhou. From here you can make a 30-minute walk to Maomaohe village, home of the Long-Skirt Miao, an ethnic sub-group.

73E2
A five-minute ferry ride from Xiamen City, Fujian Province
Seafood restaurants on the main street (£–££)
Electric buses on island
Xiamen Station
Ferry from the pier opposite Xiamen's Lujiang Hotel. Ferry tours along the coast.
Xiamen Airport
Free; island attractions: cheap

GULANGYU ISLAND ○○

Gulangyu served as the headquarters for Zheng Chenggong, the pirate-cum-Ming Dynasty loyalist who drove the Dutch from Taiwan in the 1600s. Foreigners keen to get a foothold in China settled on the island following the First Opium War (1839–1842). The main attraction here are the elaborate mansions built by Europeans after 1842.

Sunlight Rock offers terrific views of the island and its colonial architecture. The Zheng Chenggong Museum houses a collection of historical relics and weapons from the days of Zheng's rule. The Piano Museum has a collection of old pianos from around the world. Take a walk through the bustling main streets and winding alleys, packed with seafood restaurants, old architecture and shops selling local products.

HONG KONG (► 18, TOP TEN)

DID YOU KNOW?

Some 500 million people live and work along the banks of the Yangzi River.

LIJIANG (► 20–21, TOP TEN)

MACAU   ○○
The Portuguese leased Macau from China in 1557, and administered it until 1999, when it was returned to China. Once a booming trade port the small island was later eclipsed by nearby Hong Kong. Macau today is a mixture of quaint Portuguese architecture, with interesting ruins of old forts and churches as well as well-preserved colonial mansions. The island is famous for its excellent Portuguese cuisine. Don't miss the façade of St Paul's Cathedral, the symbol of Macau, or Avenida de Almeida Ribeiro, Macau's old tiled square with fountains, colonnades and old Portuguese architecture. **The Maritime Museum** is a wonderful showcase of the island's rich maritime history. Try your luck at the casinos, open 24 hours a day, or at the horse or dog race tracks.

✚ 73D1
✉ 60km west of Hong Kong
🍴 Excellent Portuguese restaurants
🚢 Regular ferries and hydrofoils from Hong Kong
❓ Macau Arts Festival, March
✈ Macau International Airport
Maritime Museum
✉ Opposite the A-Ma Temple
🕐 Daily except Tue
✋ Moderate

QUANZHOU   ○○
Once China's most important port in the Song and Yuan Dynasties, exporting spices, silk, porcelain and other goods. Tens of thousands of Arab traders began to settle here in the Tang Dynasty, when they called it Zaytun. Quanzhou flourished until the harbour silted up in the Ming Dynasty. Marco Polo visited Quanzhou, and wrote of the 'splendid city' as one of the largest ports in the world.

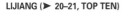

The interesting **Grand Mosque**, built in the early 11th century, is still busy with Muslim worshippers. **Kaiyuan Temple**, built in the 7th century, is famous for its stone carvings, Buddhist architecture and Song sculpture. The temple also has twin pagodas, one first built in 865 and the other in 916, but both have been renovated on numerous occasions. Within the grounds of the temple is the **Ancient Boat Exhibition**, which houses the remains of a Song ship excavated in 1973. The ship, which had sails of woven bamboo, was returning to China when it sank, and many of the goods it was carrying during the voyage were salvaged and are on display.

✚ 73E2
✉ Fujian Province
🍴 Anji Baozai Restaurant (£)
🚌 Buses to Fuzhou, Guangzhou, Shanghai, Xiamen

Grand Mosque
✉ Tumen Jie
🕐 Daily 8–6
🚌 3, 4, 5, 6, 7, 8, 9, 16
✋ Cheap

Kaiyuan Temple
✉ Xi Jie
🕐 Daily 8–5:30
🚌 2, 6, 24, 26
✋ Cheap

Ancient Boat Exhibition
✉ Xi Jie
🕐 Daily 9–5:30
🚌 2, 6, 24, 26
✋ Cheap

Dragon dancer, Macau

75

In the Know

If you only have a short time to visit China, or would like to get a real flavour of the country — here are some ideas:

Men playing draughts in Fuxing Park, Shanghai

10
Ways to be 'Chinese'

See an acrobatic show, an old Chinese folk tradition.

Get a foot or traditional massage, believed to be a cure for all sorts of ailments.

Spend an evening at a karaoke, singing your favourite songs.

Sip some *bai jiu*, China's popular sorghum spirit.

Watch a Peking Opera performance. This 200-year old art form encompasses singing, dancing, acting and acrobatics.

Take in a Chinese movie, with English subtitles, at the Cherry Lane Theatre or at one of the many other big city cinemas.

Relax in a quaint tea house. Enjoy tea brewed in the traditional way in the ambience of ancient architecture.

Enjoy a contemporary Chinese art exhibit at the Red Gate Gallery in one of the few remaining old city wall towers of Beijing.

Walk along the path of the Old Imperial Wall, lined with hundreds of species of plants and flowers, where you can examine the foundations of the original wall.

Listen to traditional Chinese music. Take in performances by some of China's best musicians at the San Wei Tea House Beijing (Saturdays only).

10
Places to Have Lunch

King Roast Duck Restaurant (££) ✉ 24 Jianguomenwai Dajie, Beijing ☎ (010) 6515 6908. Traditional Peking roast duck cooked in fruit wood heated ovens.

Lao Hanzi (££) ✉ Shichahai East Bank, Beijing ☎ (010) 6404 2259. The hearty dishes of China's Hakka minority served on the scenic banks of Shichahai.

South Silk Road (££) ✉ 3rd Fl, Building D, Soho (Xiandaicheng), Beijing ☎ (010) 8580 4286. Spicy, earthy Yunnan food served in a hip restaurant owned by Chinese artists.

Yang's Kitchen (££) ✉ No. 9 Hengshan Lu, Alley 3, Shanghai ☎ (021) 6445 8418. Shanghai-style cooking in home-like surroundings.

M on the Bund (£££) ✉ 7/F, 20 Guangdong Lu, Shanghai ☎ (021) 6350 9988. Excellent Western cuisine served up with one of the most beautiful views of the Bund (closed for lunch on Mondays).

An elaborate kite by the Bund, Shanghai

Chen Mapo Doufu Dian (£)
✉ 197 Xiyulong Jie, Chengdu, Sichuan ☎ (028) 675 4512. Home of Sichuan's famous spicy *mapo doufu* and a wide variety of other popular Sichuan snacks.

Sakura Café (£)
✉ 123 Cuiwenduan, Xinhua Lu, Old Town, Lijiang, Yunnan ☎ (0888) 518 7619. Good Western, Chinese, Korean and Japanese food is served up at this Korean-run restaurant, with outdoor seating along a beautiful section of the canal.

Laosun Jia (££)
✉ 364 Dongda Jie, Xi'an, Shaanxi ☎ (026) 721 0936. Popular Shaanxi and Muslim dishes, including the famous *yangrou paomo*, bread and lamb cooked in a tasty broth.

The Sampan (£££)
✉ Main Street, Yung Shue Wan, Lamma Island, Hong Kong. Enjoy fresh seafood *al fresco* overlooking the picturesque Lamma Harbour.

Pousada De Sao Tigao Macau (£££) ✉ Avenida da Republica, Fortaleza de Sao Tiago da Barra, Macau ☎ (853) 378 111. Tasty Portuguese cuisine overlooking the Pearl River. This hotel is the former Fortaleza da Barra, a fortress build in the 17th century by the Portuguese.

10 Top Activities

Walking – Explore Beijing's *hutongs*, old alleyways lined with traditional houses.

Taiqiquan – an ancient slow form of Chinese exercise that is practised early in the morning in parks.

Ballroom dancing – another early morning outdoor activity in parks.

Museum hopping – Visit some of the museums showcasing Chinese history and culture.

Bowling – A very popular activity among local Chinese.

Shopping – for local products and handicrafts in local markets.

Birdwatching – In the spring and fall in Beidaihe on the northeast coast of China.

Cycling – Still the way many Chinese get around, and a good way to see the city up close. Bike rentals available at most hotels.

Visit a park – Spend a few hours walking around one of the large parks that can be found in all cities, watching Chinese hard at play.

Go fly a kite – Buy a traditional Chinese kite and let fly in Tiananmen Square.

Trekking – along the Great Wall. Try the

10 Adventure Activities

challenging four-hour walk along some of the ruins that run from Simatai to Jinshanling, two and a half hours outside Beijing.

Skiing – Take to the slopes in Yabuli, Heilongjiang Province, in China's far northeast.

Hiking – Take a vigorous hike up one of China's many scenic mountains. Popular destinations are Huangshan, Taishan, Emeishan and Wutaishan.

Ice skate – rub elbows with a mass of Chinese skaters moving in every direction in Houhai.

Horse riding – Take to the trails in the grasslands of Inner Mongolia or Tibet.

Mountain biking – through the colourful countryside around Yangshuo, Dali or Lijiang

Paragliding – out at the Ming Tombs reservoir or on the Singing Sand Dunes.

Sand-sledding – on the Singing Sand Dunes at Dunhuang

Camel riding – up and down Dunhuang's Singing Sand Dunes.

Canoeing – paddle down the Li River to Yangshuo.

Chinese acrobats performing amazing feats

WUYI SHAN (WUYI MOUNTAIN) ✪✪

A two-hour trip on a bamboo raft floating downstream from Star Village is the best way to tour the Wuyi Mountain area in Fujian Province. The journey takes you down Nine-Twist Stream past peaks, cliffs, unique rock formations, bamboo groves and waterfalls The river is also known for the boat-shaped coffins sitting in depressions on the cliffs, said to belong to the Yue, a people who lived here some 3,500 years ago. Zhu Xi, the Song Dynasty Confucian scholar, lived on Wuyi Mountain for many years and founded the Ziyang Academy below Yinping Peak.

Wuyi Nature Reserve has a wide variety of flora and fauna and is also a great place for birdwatching.

✚ 73F3
✉ Northwest Fujian Province
🕒 6:30–6:30
🚆 Daily from Fuzhou, Quanzhou, Xianmen
✋ Expensive
ℹ CITS office ✉ 35 Qijianjing Lu ☎ (0599) 525 0380

XISHUANGBANNA ✪✪

Located in a subtropical region in southwest Yunnan Province, Xishuangbanna borders on Burma and Laos. According to the Dai, the main minority people here, Xishuangbanna was discovered thousands of years ago by hunters chasing golden deer. When the Mongols invaded China in the 13th century, the Dai fled south to this area, which was soon made part of the Chinese empire. Still, they managed to retain their own language and customs.

Jinghong, the capital of the Xishuangbanna Dai Autonomous Prefecture, is a jumping off point for trips to surrounding stilt villages. The most important annual event is the Water Splashing Festival in mid-April, celebrating the Dai New Year.

✚ 72B1
✉ Lao Myanmar borders, southern Yunnan Province
🍴 Dai-style food in Jinghong
🚌 Buses to Kunming
❓ Tan Ta Festival, late Oct–early Nov (rockets and hot-air balloons)
✈ Jinghong International Airport (5km south of town)

Dai Temple, Mengla, Xishuangbanna, Yunnan Province

YANGSHUO (► 24, TOP TEN)

YONGDING   ✪✪

The countryside in Yongding, Fujian Province, is dotted with circular fortress-type houses built 300 years ago by the Hakka, a Han ethnic minority, to protect themselves from attack. Many Hakka families still live in these *yuanlou* (round houses), also known as *tulou* (earth houses). The *tulous* are simple but solid buildings made of packed earth. The largest can house up to 40 families. Each building comes with a hall, kitchen, storehouse, bedrooms and a well for water.

The Hakka, or 'guest people', have their own dialect and customs. Unlike Han women, Hakka women never bound their feet, and have been more independent than other Chinese women.

The county was named Yongding, 'forever settled', at the end of Ming Dynasty, when Hakkas fled here to escape from war. About 20,000 *tulou* remain in the countryside, providing a startling sight when spotted from mountain roads above. Some of the finest examples of *tulou* architecture are **Chengqilou**, Qiaofulou, Zhengfulou, and Huaijilou. The best way to view Hakka architecture is to hire a car and driver in the city of Yongding and head out to the countryside.

ZHANGZHOU   ✪

This was a busy port city until its tidal creek silted up. The city is today known for its tropical fruits, handicrafts and local opera troupes. The **Nanshan Temple**, a popular Buddhist monastery, has a vegetarian restaurant that's open to visitors. **Hundred Flowers Village**, a botanical garden established in the Ming Dynasty, has a collection of flowers and miniature trees, better known by their Japanese name, *bonsai*.

🚆 73E2
✉ Southwest Fujian Province
🚌 Regular buses from Guangzhou, Xiamen. Minibuses from Yongding to Chengqilou

Chengqilou
✉ A 30 minute taxi ride north of Yongding
🕐 Daily
✋ Cheap

🚆 73E2
✉ Southwest Fujian Province
🚌 Regular buses from Guangzhou, Xiamen. Minibuses from Yongding to Chengqilou

Nanshan Temple
✉ Nanshan Lu
🕐 Daily 8–8
🚌 13
✋ Cheap

Hundred Flowers Village
✉ Longhai, Jiuhuzhen
🕐 Daily 8–6
🚌 13
✋ Free

Hakka women of Yongding

79

Northwest China & Tibet

Exotic Northwest China includes rich cultures and a wide variety of topographies. There are ancient Buddhist sites, mystical mountains and beautiful nature reserves in Sichuan, China's largest province. Magical Tibet has huge Buddhist monasteries and magnificent natural scenery. A rich Buddhist and Muslim heritage can be found in Gansu and Xinjiang Provinces, where you can visit oasis cities along the ancient Silk Road, a route once travelled by camel caravans carrying goods between China and the imperial courts of Rome, Arabia and India.

Known as the 'Roof of the World', Tibet is located on the vast, windswept Qinghai-Tibet Plateau, at an average 4,060m above sea level.

*' The Tibetan lads and
Western boys blend their
chants and songs,
They broil yaks whole and
cook wild camels... '*

Ts'en Ts'an
Tang Poet, c AD 745

———————•———————

Huge Buddhist prayer flag, Gyantse, Tibet

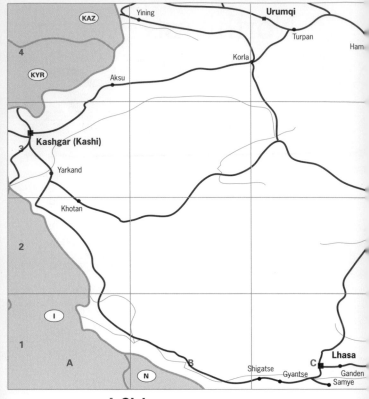

Map labels: KAZ, Yining, **Urumqi**, Turpan, Ham, Korla, KYR, Aksu, **Kashgar (Kashi)**, Yarkand, Khotan, I, N, A, B, Shigatse, Gyantse, C, **Lhasa**, Ganden, Samye

Sichuan

One of China's oldest and most populated provinces, Sichuan is home to 100 million people. Situated in the fertile Sichuan Basin, it is also the country's largest agricultural area.

What to See in Sichuan

CHENGDU

The capital of Sichuan Province is one of China's fastest growing cities, combining modern, tree-lined avenues with older areas of traditional, half-timbered houses. One such traditional house is **Du Fu's Thatched Cottage**. Du Fu (712–770), one of China's greatest poets, retired here in 759, writing 240 poems during his three-year stay. In the Song Dynasty, a thatched cottage was erected on the site of the original cottage, and was later expanded to include a garden. Du Fu wrote about the cottage in one of his poems: 'My thatched cottage is wrecked by the autumn wind'. The garden surrounding the cottage shrine is

83E1
Capital of Sichuan Province
Express buses to Chongqing, Leshan
Daily from Chongqing, Beijing, Guangzhou, Kunming, Shanghai, Xi'an
CITS office ✉ 65 Renminnan Lu ☎ (028) 8665 8731
Shangliu Airport

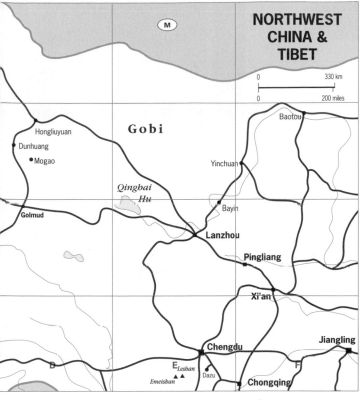

NORTHWEST CHINA & TIBET

0   330 km

0   200 miles

M

Gobi

Hongliuyuan

Dunhuang

●Mogao

Baotou

Yinchuan

Qinghai Hu

Golmud

Bayin

Lanzhou

Pingliang

Xi'an

Jiangling

Chengdu

E *Lesban*

Emeishan ▲ ▲

Dazu

Chongqing

planted with different types of bamboo, making it a pleasant place for a stroll. There is also a teahouse in the garden. **Wenshu Yuan**, also known as **Manjusiri Temple**, was founded in the 6th century and is the headquarters of Chan (Zen) Buddhism in China. The temple, which is dedicated to the God of Wisdom, was destroyed in fighting during the Ming Dynasty, and rebuilt in 1691. It has more than 100 bronze Buddhas produced by well-known craftsmen. The complex also has a tea house and vegetarian restaurant. The bustling street in front of the temple is also worth visiting, with its fortune-tellers and peddlers selling incense, candles, prayer beads, ghost money and other religious paraphernalia.

Also worth visiting is **Wuhou Ci**, a series of memorial halls dedicated to Zhu Geliang, a military genius of the State of Shu immortalised in the Chinese classic, *The Romance of the Three Kingdoms*. The temple was founded in the fifth century, but was rebuilt in 1672, and was recently restored. The site displays three bronze drums, purportedly used by the Shu army under Zhu.

Du Fu's Thatched Cottage
- ✉ Ximenwai
- 🕐 Daily 7–6:30
- 🚌 301

Wenshu Yuan (Manjusiri Temple)
- ✉ 15 Wenshuyuan Jie
- 🕐 Daily 8–9
- 🚌 55, 64
- 💰 Cheap

Wuhou Ci
- ✉ 231 Wuhouci Dajie
- 🕐 Daily 0–7
- 🚌 1, 8, 19, 53, 57, 82, 301, 302
- 💰 Moderate

A souvenir stall in Chongqing

CHONGQING (CHUNGKING) ⊗

The hilly city of Chongqing has a history going back more than 2,000 years. It was the capital of the ancient state of Ba in the Zhou Dynasty. The city was named an open treaty port in 1890, but attracted little foreign interest. Chongqing, which is known for its stifling summers, has earned a place on the list of China's four 'furnaces'. **Hongyan Cun** or **Red Crag Village** served as the offices and residences for the Communist representatives during the alliance with the Nationalists during the fight against the Japanese. It was also the headquarters of the Eighth Route Army. The site has an excellent modern museum illustrating the history of revolution in China beginning with the 1911 overthrow of the Qing. Unfortunately, there are no explanations in English also in the city, **The US-Chiang Kaishek Criminal Acts Exhibition Hall** and **SACO Prison** commemorates the jail set up by the notorious Dai Li, founder of the infamous Blue Shirts, a Nationalist organisation. The grim prison held hundreds of political prisoners under very harsh conditions. Short dramatic performances are held throughout the day, telling the stories of famous prisoners once incarcerated there.

DID YOU KNOW?

The image of an endless cycle, the 'Wheel of Life', is generally found at the entrance to Tibetan monasteries.

DAZU ✪✪

The Dazu Buddhist Caves, 160km northwest of Chongqing, Sichuan Province, are divided among 40 different locations, and include more than 50,000 carvings from the Tang and Song Dynasties. This is one of the most important Buddhist archaeological sites in China, predating other such sites by hundreds of years. The two most popular caves are Beishan and Baodingshan, each of which has around 10,000 sculptures.

The sculptures in Baodingshan, 15km northeast of Dazu, are said to be the most beautiful. They were made during the Southern Song Dynasty, and are scattered around 13 different sites. The sculptures were paid for with funds raised by Zhao Zhifeng, a monk who turned Baodingshan into a centre of Tantric Buddhism. Cave 8 is home to the largest 1,000-armed Buddha in China, which has an eye in each of its palms. The Great Buddha Crescent, some 500m long, is the site of the most famous Buddha at Dazu, the Reclining Buddha entering Nirvana, which stretches 31m from head to knees.

Beishan, just 2km north of Dazu, has 290 caves. The sculptures here were produced in the Tang Dynasty. This was a former military stronghold held by Wei Junjing, a Sichuan military leader who ordered the construction of the first Buddhist temple at Beishan. Cave 136, the best preserved and largest of the caves, shows Puxian, the patron deity of Mount Emei, riding a white elephant, and several representations of Guanyin, the God- dess of Mercy. It also has a large carved wheel representing the cycle of life and death. Cave 125 has a large sculpture of Guanyin. Cave 245 has an inter- esting reproduction of the Western Paradise ruled by the Amitabha, with more than 1,000 small carvings. A pagoda sits on the top of the mountain.

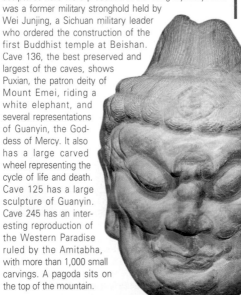

The head of a lokapala, or temple guardian, Tang period

✚ 83E1
✉ 160km northwest of Chongqing, Chongqing Municipality
🍴 Street foodstalls on Shizi Jie
🚌 Daily to Chengdu, Chongqing

Baodinsan
✉ Baoding Zhen
🕐 8:30–5:30
🚌 Take a long distance bus from Chongqing
✋ Moderate

Beishan
✉ Baoding Zhen, Beishan
🕐 8:30–5:30
🚌 Take a long distance bus from Chongqing
✋ Moderate

EMEISHAN (MT EMEI) ✪✪

83E1

6.5km west of Emei Town, 35km west of Leshan, Sichuan Province

Teddy Bear Café (£)

Regular buses between Leshan and Emei Town

Daily from Chengdu, Kunming

Expensive

Emeishan International Travel Service

Mingshandong Lu

(0842) 552 7555

One of China's four sacred Buddhist Mountains, Emeishan represents Puxian, the Bodhisattva of Universal Kindness, usually seen riding a white elephant. Emeishan is covered with bamboo, fir trees, pine trees and a variety of plants and flowers, and has a wide variety of butterflies, birds, monkeys, and pandas.

There are two trails up the mountain, which at 3,000m can be a rough climb. The northern route is shorter and more direct, while the southern route is longer and more strenuous. Wannian Temple is the usual starting place. There are about 30 temples on the mountain, the most famous of which is Baoguo Temple, considered the gateway to Emeishan.

The walk up and down the mountain can take two to four days, but there are hostels along the way to break up the trip. The mountain is popular and can be crowded with tourists, so be sure to make reservations in advance. For those seeking an easier way up the mountain there are buses running to a point half way up, where you can transfer to a cable car after a short walk.

LESHAN ✪✪

83E1

115km south of Chengdu, Sichuan Province

Restaurants along Xuedao Jie

Regular buses to Chengdu, Chongqing

Moderate

Tour boats for the Giant Buddha leave from Leshan pier every 30 minutes, 7AM–5PM

Detail of Leshan Buddha

Carved in the face of a cliff in the Tang Dynasty, the Maitreya Buddha in Leshan gazes calmly over the confluence of the Min, Dadu and Qingyi rivers.

The statue, which is said to have taken 90 years to complete, is the largest carved stone Buddha in the country. It is known in Chinese simply as Dafo, or the Big Buddha. The seated statue is 71m tall. The head alone is 14.7m, the ears 7m long, and it is said that one could hold a picnic on the nail of its big toe.

The statue can be viewed by boat from the river, or by climbing to the top of the hill next to where the statue stands and then descending the steps to its foot.

YANGZI JIANG (YANGTZE RIVER) (➤ 25, TOP TEN)

Gansu & Xinjiang

Gansu is a large, but sparsely populated desert province. The Xinjiang Uighur Autonomous Region is the largest province of China. The population is primarily Muslim Turkic-speaking peoples from Central Asia.

What to See in Gansu and Xinjiang

Uighur carpet sellers, Kashg[

KASHGAR ✪✪✪

Kashgar, located in the Xinjiang Autonomous Region near the border with Pakistan, is the westernmost town in China. The city, which opened to foreign visitors in 1985, remains primarily Central Asian, with little Chinese flavour.

In ancient times, Kashgar was one of the most important oasis towns on the Silk Road between the Middle East and China. The opening of the Karakorum Highway linking China and Pakistan in 1986 bolstered the city's position as an important transport hub.

Some 150,000 people visit the Sunday Market, just 2km from the centre of town, each Sunday to purchase metal ware, jewellery, rugs, pottery, musical instruments and spices as well as to sample traditional Central Asian specialities, such as nan bread and mutton kebabs. Centrally located, the **Id Kah Mosque** is one of the largest mosques in China. It is believed to have been built in 1738, and was later renovated several times. The main hall can accommodate about 7,000 worshippers.

In an eastern suburb of Kashgar stands the **Mausoleum of Abakh Hoja** – a Muslim holy man – and five generations of his family. This domed structure is also said to be the burial place of Xiangfei, a beautiful concubine of the Qing Emperor Qianlong, believed to be Abakh Hoja's daughter.

✚ 82A3
✉ Xinjiang Province, Western China
🍴 Uighur foodstalls outside the Id Kah Mosque
🚌 Buses to Kyrgyzstan, Pakistan and Urumqi
🚆 Daily from Urumqi
✈ Kashgar Airport (12km northeast of town, but very few flights)

Mausoleum of Abakh Hoja
✉ Aizilaiti Lu
🕐 8:30AM–5PM
💵 Cheap

Id Kah Mosque
✉ Jiefang Beilu, west of Id Kah Square
🕐 9AM–5PM
💵 Cheap

DID YOU KNOW?

More than 18,680 precious stones were used to decorate the stupa of the 5th Dalai Lama.

MOGAO KU (MOGAO CAVES) (▶ 22, TOP TEN)

TURPAN (TURFAN OR TULUFAN) ✪✪

Once a major oasis town on the Silk Road between China and the Middle East, Turpan was once also an important Buddhist centre, until migrations of Uighurs, a Turkic-speaking people, brought the area under the influence of Islam in the 8th century.

Turpan is today an agricultural centre famous for sweet Hami melons, dates and grapes, which are made into wine. Underground irrigation channels bring melted snow

🕂 82C4
✉ 165km east of Urumqi, Xinjiang Province
🍴 John's Information Café (£)
🚌 Buses to Urumqi, minibuses to Daheyan
🚉 Daheyan Station 58km north of Turpan

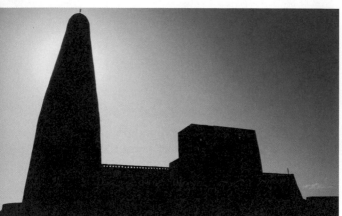

Emin minaret in Turfan silhouetted against setting sun

to the city from the edge of the Tianshan Mountain Range. The town, in the Xinjiang Uighur Autonomous Region, has extreme temperature variations. The city is also known as the Land of Fire, due to its intense summer heat, which can reach 40°C. Winter temperatures can reach a low of -5°C. Turpan is 60 percent Uighur and about 10 percent Hui. Many famous 20th century Western explorers and archaeologists came here to explore the ancient caves, including Sir Aurel Stein, and they shipped crates of sculptures, frescoes and numerous other treasures and artefacts to Europe.

The city has a busy Sunday bazaar, where colourful silk dresses and hats are a speciality. The circular Emin Minaret, at the Suleiman Mosque, was built in 1777 using unglazed mud bricks in the Afghan style. **Bezeklik**, located in the mountains outside the city, is a Buddhist cave with deteriorated carvings made between the 5th and 14th centuries, and Tang frescoes.

Bezeklik
✉ Northwest side of the Flaming Mountains
🕐 Daily 9–5
💷 Moderate

Tibet & Qinghai

Tibetan culture prospered during the 10th to 16th centuries. In the 18th century, China made Tibet a protectorate, and began to control the Dalai Lamas. Tibet became relatively independent after the 1911 revolution, but was seized by China in 1951 by soldiers of the People's Liberation Army.

What to See in Tibet & Qinghai

GANDEN GOMPA (GANDEN MONASTERY)   ✪

Ganden Monastery, built in the early 15th century by Tsongkhapa, is today home to several hundred Buddhist monks. The monastery was seriously damaged during the Cultural Revolution, but renovations have been carried out in recent years. A stupa at the monastery holds the remains of Tsongkhapa

- 🔲 82C1
- ✉ 45km east of Lhasa
- 🕐 9AM–5PM
- ✋ Cheap

GYANTSE   ✪✪

Travellers to Shigatse often stop off at Gyantse, situated at the juncture of two important caravan routes to India and Nepal. The city, Tibet's fourth largest, was important strategically, and was once a major trading centre for nomads. The **Palkhor Monastery**, built in the 1427, has been badly damaged, but is worth visiting, especially its Nepalese Kumbun stupa with painted eyes and beautiful murals. The city's old fort, or Dzong, which overlooks the city, was hit by British artillery in 1904 and again by the People's Liberation Army in 1960.

LHASA (► 19, TOP TEN)

- 🔲 82C1
- ✉ 255km southwest of Lhasa, Tibet
- 🍴 Wutse Restaurant (£)
- 🚌 Minibuses from Lhasa via Shigatse

Palkhor Monastery
- ✉ Gyantse
- ✋ Moderate

Gyantse Kumbum Monastery, Tibet

✚ 83E2
✉ 155km from Xining,
Qinghai Province
🚌 Regular buses from
Xining to Heimahe
❓ Best to book a tour to
Bird Island at a travel
agency in Xining

QINGHAI HU (QINGHAI LAKE) ✪

Qinghai Lake is a salt water lake in northeast Qinghai Province, 300km from Xining. It is the largest inland lake in China, covering an area of 4,455 sq km and with a circumference of 900km. Called the Western Sea in ancient times, the lake was formed some 1 million years ago when a fault appeared in the earth's surface. Qinghai Lake is surrounded by mountains, and more than 50 rivers run into it. It's drained by the Yellow River and its tributaries.

The lake is the largest breeding ground for birds in China, with some 12 species migrating here from India and southern China to breed from March to early June. Birds found here include wild geese, gulls, cormorants, sandpipers, and the rare black-necked cranes.

✚ 82C1
✉ Approximately 30km
west of Tsetang
✋ Cheap

SAMYE ✪

Samye Monastery, the first Buddhist monastery to be built in Tibet, was founded by an Indian scholar, the abbot Shantarakshita, during the reign of King Trisong Detsen in the 8th century.

✚ 82C1
✉ 250km southwest of
Lhasa, Tibet
🍴 Tenzin Restaurant (£)
🚌 Minibuses from Lhasa

Tashilhunpo Monastery
✉ 250km southwest of
Lhasa, Tibet
🍴 Tenzin Restaurant (£)
🚌 Minibuses from Lhasa

SHIGATSE ✪✪

Located in the valley of the Yarlong Tsangpo River, or the Brahmaputra, Shigatse is the second largest urban area in Tibet. It once rivalled Lhasa as a spiritual and political centre. The noble families of this once wealthy city founded many monasteries. The city was dominated by the Red Hat Sect until the arrival of the fifth Dalai Lama, who defeated the sect with the support of the Mongolians, uniting the country under the Yellow Hat Sect.

The beautiful **Tashilhunpo Monastery**, the seat of the Panchen Lama, was built here in 1447. The terraced monastery has a 28m statue of the Maitreya Buddha and a Grand Hall that houses the tomb of the fourth Panchen Lama. The monastery is also well known for its mandalas, or meditation pictures, made with coloured sands.

*Yak and rider on the high
Tibetan plateau*

Where To...

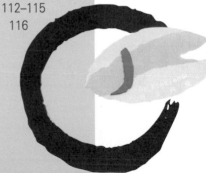

Above: *The atrium of the Grand Hyatt Hotel, Shanghai*
Right: *Restaurant sign, Xintiandi, Shanghai*

Northern China

Prices
Average prices for a meal for two excluding drinks:
£ = under 100 yuan
££ = 100–250 yuan
£££ = over 250 yuan

Beijing

Afunti (££)
Uighur cuisine from China's far-flung Xinjiang Province. Specialities include tender legs of lamb, lamb kebabs, sesame coated lamb strips, and Xinjiang salad accompanied by tasty naan bread.
✉ 2A Houguaibang Hutong, Chaonei Dajie ☎ (010) 6527 2288 🕐 Lunch, dinner

Beijing Roast Duck Restaurant (££)
A simple restaurant where Beijing families go to enjoy authentic Peking duck.
✉ Building 3, Tuanjiehu Beikou ☎ (010) 6582 2892 🕐 Lunch, dinner

Donglaishun (££)
Muslim-style hot pot. Cook meat and vegetables in a boiling broth at your own table, and then dunk the cooked portions into a special sauce.
✉ 44 Dongjiaomin Xiang ☎ (010) 6524 1042 🕐 Lunch, dinner

Fangshan Restaurant (£££)
This restaurant serves imperial dishes favoured by the old Manchu rulers. Located in a beautiful setting along a lake in Beihai Park.
✉ 1 Wenjin Jie, inside the south gate of Beihai Park ☎ (010) 6401 1889 🕐 Lunch, dinner

Golden Cat Dumpling City (£)
Dumplings served with a wide variety of fillings, from traditional pork, lamb and beef, fish to pumpkin, eggplant, some mixed with dill, fennel and chives.
✉ East gate of Tuanjiehu Park ☎ (010) 8598 5011 🕐 Lunch, dinner

Gongdelin Vegetarian Restaurant (££)
The capital's most famous vegetarian restaurant, serving non-meat dishes that look and taste like the real thing.
✉ 158 Qianmennan Dajie ☎ (010) 6702 0867 🕐 Lunch, dinner

Jin Shan Cheng (£)
One of the best Sichuan restaurants Beijing. Try gongbao chicken, *ganbian tudou* (a tasty potato dish) and *mapo* bean curd.
✉ Zhongfu Building, Third Ring Road ☎ (010) 6581 6688 ext 2131 🕐 Lunch, dinner

Kong Yiji (££)
Tastefully designed restaurant, with Zhejiang specialities. Sample lima beans (*huixiangdou*), smelly bean curd (*choudoufu*), beef with cruller (*niurou youtiao*), washed down with Shaoxing wine, a grain alcohol heated in a metal server.
✉ 322 Dongsibei Dajie ☎ (010) 6404 0507 🕐 Lunch and dinner

The Hakka Restaurant (££)
Sample the cuisine of China's 'guest people', the Hakkas. Try tasty *meicai kourou* (fatty pork with preserved vegetables) or *zhuyan xia* (shrimp cooked in rock salt).
✉ Beside Shichahai, 20m north of Pingan Dadao facing the east side of the lake. ☎ (010) 6404 2259 🕐 Lunch, dinner

Red Capital Club (£££)

Excellent Chinese cuisine served in a beautifully restored courtyard house. The dishes are said to be the favourites of China's top leaders. The bar is decorated with Cultural Revolution artefacts.

✉ 66 Dongsi Jiutiao, Dongcheng district ☎ (010) 6402 7150 🕔 Dinner only

Xiaowangfu (££)

Tasty home-style cooking served in a friendly neighbourhood restaurant.

✉ 2 Guanghuadongli ☎ (010) 6591 3255 🕔 Lunch, dinner

Chengde

Imperial City Restaurant (££)

Wild game popular with the Qing emperors, such as wild deer, rabbit and pheasant.

✉ 98 Xiaonanmen, outside Dehuimen Gate, the Imperial Villa ☎ (0314) 202 5757 🕔 Lunch, dinner

Datong

Tongheyuan Hotpot Restaurant (££)

Typical hotpot restaurant. Cook meat, vegetables and bean curd in a steaming broth right at your own table.

✉ Beside the Feitian Hotel ☎ (0352) 280 3111 🕔 Lunch, dinner

Yongho Hongqi Restaurant (££)

This slightly (for Datong) upmarket restaurant offers a wide variety of Chinese dishes. Picture menu makes ordering easier.

✉ 3 Yingbin Lu ☎ (0352) 510 3008 🕔 Lunch, dinner

Harbin

Dongfang Dumpling King (£)

Tasty northern-style dumplings with a wide variety of fillings.

✉ 39 Zhongyang Dajie ☎ (0415) 469 0888 🕔 Lunch, dinner

Huamei Xicanting (£)

Sample Russian cuisine here.

✉ 112 Zhongyang Dajie (opposite the Modern Hotel) ☎ (0415) 467 5574 🕔 Lunch, dinner

Pingyao

Yunjingcheng Binguan (£)

Simple Shanxi dishes including fried buns stuffed with meat (*jianbao*), or the local noodles in this small courtyard restaurant and hotel.

✉ Mingqing Dajie ☎ (0354) 568 0944 🕔 Lunch, dinner

Tianjin

Goubuli (£)

This restaurant, which dates back 100 years, specialises in *baozi* (steamed buns) filled with pork, chicken or shrimp, with spices.

✉ 77 Shandong Lu ☎ (022) 2730 0810 🕔 Lunch, dinner

Xi'an

Laosunjia Restaurant (££)

This well-known restaurant specialises in Muslim and Xi'an dishes, including *yangrou paomo*, bread and lamb cooked in broth.

✉ 364 Dongda Jie ☎ (029) 721 0936 🕔 Lunch, Dinner

Alcoholic Drinks

Virtually all restaurants in China – unless they are Muslim – serve alcohol in the form of beer or rice wine. Imported spirits and wines are usually only available at more up-market restaurants and bars.

Eastern China

Beverages

While tea is the standard beverage served at meals, restaurants also serve a wide variety of soft drinks, mineral waters, juices, and alcoholic beverages, including an increasingly wide variety of wines in better establishments. Chinese are serious beer drinkers, and just about every town has at least one brewery, so when travelling, try the local brews. A Chinese favourite is *baijiu*, a grain-based, potent beverage.

Hangzhou

Louwailou (££)

Located with excellent views of West Lake. Specialities include West Lake vinegar fish (*xihu cuyu*), *dongpo rou* (pork slices cooked with Shaoxing wine), longjing shrimp and beggar's chicken.
✉ 39 Gushan Lu ☎ (0571) 796 9023 ⓘ Lunch, dinner

Tianwaitian Restaurant (£££)

Popular Chinese dishes served in the two main dining floors. Or try the wonton and noodles at the Tianwaitian Snack Annex.
✉ 2 Tianzhu Lu ☎ (0571) 796 5450 ⓘ Breakfast, lunch and dinner

Zhiweiguan Restaurant (£)

This simple restaurant offers popular local snacks from noodles to boiled and steamed dumplings. Try cat's ears (not what you think) – small triangles of dough snipped off into a boiling pot, and served in a broth.
✉ 83 Renhe Lu ☎ (0571) 506 3055 ⓘ Breakfast, lunch and dinner

Luoyang

One of a Kind Restaurant (£)

A variety of inexpensive local specialities.
✉ 359 Zhongzhou Lu ☎ (0379) 399 1404 ⓘ Lunch, dinner

Nanjing

Spring Garden at the Dingshan (££)

Considered by some to be the best restaurant in Nanjing, this restaurant serves popular Nanjing dishes.
✉ Dingshan Guest House, 90 Chahaer Lu 4(025) 880 1868 ⓘ Lunch, dinner

Wanqing Lou

Nanjing set dinner with 20 small dishes.
✉ Opposite side of the Qinhuai River in the area of the Confucius Temple (Fuzimiao) ☎ (025) 2249877 ⓘ Lunch, dinner

Putuoshan

Baihua Teahouse (£)

Vegetarian dishes made to taste and resemble meat dishes.
✉ 6 Xianghua Jie ☎ (0580) 609 1208 ⓘ Breakfast, lunch and dinner

Wanghai Restaurant (£)

Serves up Putuoshan specialities. This is the place where the island locals dine out.
✉ Beside the Fayu Temple ☎ (0580) 609 1671 ⓘ Breakfast, lunch and dinner

Qingdao

Chunhe Restaurant (£)

Traditional Qingdao seafood dishes served at one of the coastal city's most popular restaurants. Fast food served on the first floor and regular dishes on the second floor.
✉ 146 Zhongshan Lu ☎ (0532) 282 7371 ⓘ Lunch, dinner

Shanghai

30s (£££)

A restaurant with a 1930s theme owned by a group of

well known Shanghai artists, playwrights and poets. 30s serves up creative dishes not commonly found in other restaurants.

✉ 134 Nanyang Lu, Jingan District ☎ (021) 6256 2265 🕔 Lunch, dinner

Huxingting Tea House (£)

Serves Shanghai snacks and tea.

✉ 257 Yuyuan Lu ☎ (021) 6373 6950 🕔 Lunch, dinner

Lu Lu's (££)

Once a small dive, Lu Lu's has since developed into one of Shanghai's trendiest restaurants, famous for Shanghai food.

✉ 69 Shimenyi Lu ☎ (021) 6258 5645 🕔 Lunch, dinner

M on the Bund (£££)

Good western cuisine served with one of the best views of the waterfront and the Pudong skyline. M on the Bund serves good Mediterranean cuisine and has an excellent collection of wines. Smart attire a must

✉ 7/F, 20 Guangdong Lu, Huangpu District ☎ (021) 6350 9988 🕔 Closed Mon lunch

Sasha's (££)

The renovated historic home of T.V. Song, brother-in-law of Chiang Kaishek, and financier to the Nationalists. Continental cuisine in an elegant Western setting. Western-style seafood is a speciality here.

✉ Building 11, 20 Guangping Lu, Lu Wan District ☎ (021) 6474 6166 🕔 Lunch, dinner

Xianqianfang Folk Restaurant (££)

This restaurant, which has an impressive collection of antiques, is located in an old style villa, and offers excellent Shanghai cuisine and service.

✉ 1468 Hongqiao Lu, Gubei District ☎ (021) 6295 1717 🕔 Lunch, dinner

Yang's Kitchen (££)

Shanghai home-style cooking in a refined setting.

✉ 9 Hongshan Lu, Alley 3 (near the intersection of Dongping Lu) ☎ (021) 6431 3513 🕔 Lunch, dinner

Suzhou

Songhelou (£)

The long-established Songhelou is known for its eastern Chinese seafood cooking.

✉ 18 Taijian Nong, 141 Guanqian Jie ☎ (0512) 727 7006 🕔 Lunch, dinner

Taishan

Daguanyuan Roast Duck Restaurant (££)

Inexpensive roast duck and all the trimmings.

✉ 8 Tongtian Jie ☎ (0538) 826 0664 🕔 Lunch, dinner

Wuxi

Jinxi Revolving Restaurant (££)

Enjoy an inexpensive Chinese and Western buffet as you revolve atop the Jinjiang Hotel.

✉ 219 Zhongshan Lu ☎ (0510) 275 1688 🕔 Lunch, dinner

Wuxi Roast Duck House (££)

Roast duck and Jiangsu specialities of the region.

✉ 222 Zhongshan Lu ☎ (0510) 270 8222 🕔 Lunch, dinner

Drinking Etiquette

When dining in a more formal setting, guests usually do not drink individually. It is considered polite to wait for the host or another guest to toast you before drinking from your glass. You may also offer a toast to others sitting at the table. Make eye contact with your intended target and raise your glass with two hands, tipping it slightly in his or her direction. After taking a drink, hold out the glass in the direction of the person to show how much you've consumed. It's common for Chinese friends to try to get you to drink a lot, and you will often hear the toast *ganbei*, or 'dry bottom'. If you don't like to finish your drink in a single gulp, you can just say *suiyi*, or 'how you wish', which means either party can drink as much as the person likes.

Southern China

The Timeless Taste
Soy sauce or *jiangyou* is one of the oldest known condiments in the world. When soya beans are mixed with salt, water or sometimes rice wine, their protein is broken down into amino acids which act as a stimulant to taste. Note, however, that the Chinese don't sprinkle it randomly over their rice bowls as is so often the case in the West – rather they use it as a constituent in cooking, and value it highly.

Dali

Sunshine Café (£)
Simple Western, Bai and Chinese fare served by friendly staff in a laid-back setting. Hearty breakfasts served with fresh Yunnan coffee.
✉ 16 Huguo Lu ☎ (0872) 266 0712 ⏰ Lunch, dinner

Tibet Café (£)
Good Tibetan and Western favourites, including fresh Yunnan coffee and desserts, served at a roadside café.
✉ 81 Huguo Lu ☎ (0872) 267 0598 ⏰ Breakfast, lunch and dinner

Guangzhou

Banxi Jiujia (££)
Popular dim sum delicacies and other Cantonese favourites.
✉ 151 Longjinxi Lu ☎ (020) 8181 5718 ⏰ Breakfast, lunch and dinner

Black Swan Dumpling Restaurant (£)
Northern-style dumplings as well as meat dishes, such as roast leg of lamb and deer.
✉ 486 Huanshi Lu, 2nd floor ☎ (020) 8767 5687 ⏰ Lunch, dinner

Caigenxiang Vegetarian Restaurant (££)
Shanghainese-style vegetarian cuisine
✉ 167 Zhongshanliu Lu ☎ (020) 8334 4363 ⏰ Lunch, dinner

Guangzhou Restaurant (££)
A local favourite, this old eatery specialises in seafood and the Cantonese dim sum.
✉ 2 Wenchangnan Lu ☎ (020) 8188 8388 ⏰ Breakfast, lunch and dinner

Lotus Restaurant (££)
Excellent dim sum restaurant serving Cantonese snacks and noodles from pushcarts within the restaurant.
✉ 67 Dishinan Lu ☎ (020) 8181 3388 ⏰ Breakfast, lunch and dinner

Shengji Restaurant (££)
Traditional Cantonese cuisine including exotic south China favourites such as snake.
✉ 228 Changdidama Lu ☎ (020) 8332 8318 ⏰ Lunch, dinner

Guilin

Yiyuan Restaurant (£)
Sichuan favourites served in a comfortable and clean setting. English menu available.
✉ 106 Nanhuan Lu ☎ (0773) 282 0470 ⏰ Lunch, dinner

Hong Kong

Felix (£££)
Incredible location on the 28th floor of the Peninsula Hotel serving a mix of European and Asian dishes.
✉ The Peninsula, Salisbury Road, Tsim Sha Tsui ☎ (852) 2315 3188 ⏰ Lunch, dinner

Hunan Garden (£££)
Excellent hot, spicy food from Hunan. Great selection of dumpling dishes.
✉ The Forum, Exchange Square, 8 Connaught Place, Central ☎ (852) 2868 2880 ⏰ Lunch, dinner

Lijiang

Lamu's House of Tibet (£)
This pleasant garden restaurant, built of bamboo, serves excellent Tibetan dishes.

✉ On Xinyi Jie, just past the entrance to the Old Town ☎ (0888) 518 9000 🕐 Breakfast, lunch and dinner

69 Vegetarian Restaurant (£)
Vegetarian dishes served in a rustic setting.

✉ 69 Mishi Alley, Xinyi Jie, Old Town ☎ (0888) 518 5206 🕐 Lunch and dinner

Mama Fu's (£)
Enjoy Chinese and Western dishes alfresco while sitting beside the canal. Try the apple pie for dessert.

✉ 76 Xinyi Jie, Mishi Xiang ☎ (0888) 512 2285 🕐 Lunch and dinner

Sakura Café (£)
Good Bai, Korean, Japanese and Western dishes, including hearty breakfasts. For dessert try the excellent brownies or banana or chocolate pancakes.

✉ 123 Cuiwenduan, Xinhua Lu, Old Town ☎ (0888) 518 7619 🕐 Breakfast, lunch and dinner

Quanzhou

Anji Baozai Restaurant (£)
This 24-hour restaurant offers a wide variety of Chinese snacks and dishes. Try the oven-roasted rice platter with accompanying dishes.

✉ Corner of Wenling Lu and Tumen Jie ☎ (0595) 298 299 🕐 Breakfast, lunch and dinner

Xiamen

Gulang Xinyu Restaurant (Gulangyu Island) (£££)
Excellent fresh seafood dishes.

✉ 4 Zhonghua Lu ☎ (0592) 206 3073 🕐 Breakfast, lunch and dinner

Haoxlanglai Chinese-Western Restaurant (££)
This 24-hour restaurant serves Western food, including steaks and salads. There is also a US$5 set meal, including meat, soup, vegetables, bread and beverage.

✉ 5 Haihou Lu ☎ (0592) 203 5212 🕐 Breakfast, lunch and dinner

Xishuangbana

Meimei Café (£)
Popular with backpackers, the Meimei Café serves up sandwiches, burgers and milk shakes. Also a good place to pick up local travel information.

✉ Jindexi Lu, opposite the entrance to Manting Lu, Jinghong ☎ (0691) 212 7324 🕐 Breakfast, lunch and dinner

Yangshuo

Minnie Mao's (£)
Popular with backpackers, and one of the first restaurants on Xijie, Minnie Mao's serves Western-style breakfasts, hamburgers, sandwiches and milk shakes as well as Chinese dishes.

✉ 83 Xi Jie 🕐 Breakfast, lunch and dinner

Chopsticks
While some restaurants will have knives and forks available for foreign guests, this may not always be the case, and so it's a good idea to learn how to wield a pair of chopsticks. Hold the chopsticks about two-thirds from the bottom, leaning them against the web between your thumb and index finger. Use the index and middle fingers as a fulcrum to manoeuvre the two sticks. Do not stand your chopsticks into your bowl of rice – which resembles incense placed in a bowl in a funeral service – but place them on the chopstick holder, or across your bowl. Also remember not to lay them down pointing in the direction of other guests, which is considered rude.

Northwest China

Eight Treasures Tea

A speciality of Sichuan, Eight Treasures Tea is the perfect accompaniment to spicy cuisine. The eight ingredients in the cup are jasmine, jujube, walnut, fruit of Chinese wolfberry, raisin, crystal sherry, ginseng and dried longan pulp, sweetened with rock sugar. Steaming water is added to your cup from a special brass teapot with a very long spout, pored by highly skilled tea boys from several feet away.

Chengdu

Baguo Buyi Restaurant (££)

One of Chengdu's more up-market restaurants, specialising in traditional Sichuan fare. Try the spicy *dan dan mian* (dan dan noodles)

✉ 20 Renminnan Lu, Siduan ☎ (028) 8557 3839 🕐 Lunch, dinner

Chengdu Restaurant (£)

One of Chengdu's most popular restaurants, this eatery serves authentic Sichuan dishes, with the accent on spicy hot.

✉ 134 Shangdong Jie 🕐 Lunch, dinner

Chen Mapo Doufu Restaurant (£)

Prepares the spicy bean curd dish that made Chengdu famous as well as other Sichuan peppery favourites.

✉ 197 Xiyulong Jie ☎ (028) 8675 4512 🕐 Lunch, dinner

Huangcheng Laoma Restaurant (££)

Traditional Sichuan hotpot restaurant. Order meat and vegetables and cook them in the hotpot at your own table. A variety of broths is available.

✉ 20 Qintailou Lu ☎ (028) 8613 1752 🕐 Lunch, dinner

Long Chaoshou (£–££)

Opened in 1940, this is one of Chengdu's oldest and most famous restaurants. Each of the three floors serves different types of food. The ground floor offers a wide variety of Sichuan snacks. The more up-market first-floor restaurant serves typical Sichuan favourites.

✉ 8 South Chunxi Lu ☎ (028) 8667 6345 🕐 Lunch, dinner

Sucai Restaurant (£)

Vegetarian restaurant located in the Wenshu Buddhist Monastery.

✉ Wenshu Monastery ☎ (028) 725 7507 🕐 Lunch, dinner

Dunhuang

If you're not put off by street stall food, try the bustling market to the south of Yangguan Dong Lu, nearly opposite the Dunhuang Museum, which serves a wide variety of inexpensive foods until around midnight.

Charley Johng's Café (£)

Chinese and Western food. Travel assistance – tickets, bike rentals – Internet, also available.

✉ Mingshan Lu ☎ (0937) 883 3039 🕐 Breakfast, lunch and dinner

John's Information Café (£)

The traveller's dream. In addition to food, this café provides free travel information and can arrange local trips. In addition, there's Internet access and bike rentals.

✉ 22 Mingshan Lu (Beside the Feitian Hotel) ☎ (0937) 882 7000 🕐 Breakfast, lunch and dinner

Shirley's Café (£)

Copy of Charley Johng's (Shirley is said to be his sister).

✉ Mingshan Lu, opposite Charley Johng's Café ☎ (0937) 882 6387 🕐 Breakfast, lunch and dinner

Emeishan

Teddy Bear Café (£)
Popular with backpackers, this simple restaurant serves both Western and Sichuan dishes. Travel information also available.

✉ **On the main road leading to Baoguo Monastery** ☎ **(0833) 559 0085** 🕐 **Breakfast, lunch and dinner.**

Gyantse

Wutse Restaurant (£)
Inexpensive Tibetan, Indian, Nepali and Western fare served in an interesting setting.

✉ **Wutse Hotel, Yingxiongnan Lu** ☎ **(0892) 817 2880** 🕐 **Breakfast, lunch and dinner**

Zhuangyuan Restaurant (£)
If you're looking for an alternative to Tibetan dishes, try this Sichuan eatery.

✉ **Yingxiongnan Lu, opposite the Wutse Hotel** ☎ **(0892) 817 2526** 🕐 **Breakfast, lunch and dinner**

Kashgar

John's Information Café (£)
Very popular with travellers. Serves good international food, provides reliable local information and arranges Kashgar tours.

✉ **Located at the junction of Seman Lu and Xiaminglibage Lu** ☎ **(0998) 255 1186** 🕐 **Breakfast, lunch and dinner**

Lhasa

Lightfull Restaurant (£)
Offers well-prepared Tibetan, Western and Chinese cuisine at reasonable prices.

✉ **A few steps form the Yak Hotel on Beijingdong Lu** 🕐 **Breakfast, lunch and dinner**

Snowlands Restaurant (£)
Inexpensive Chinese, Tibetan, Indian and Western dishes.

✉ **4 Zangyiyuan Lu** ☎ **(0891) 633 7323** 🕐 **Breakfast, lunch and dinner**

Tashi 2 (£)
Backpackers favourite. Typical Tibetan and Western dishes.

✉ **Kirey Hotel, 105 Beijingdong Lu** 🕐 **Breakfast, lunch and dinner**

The Third Eye (£)
Good Indian food in a relaxed setting.

✉ **74 Zangyidong Lu** 🕐 **Breakfast, lunch and dinner**

Shigatse

Tenzin Restaurant (£)
Standard Chinese and Tibetan dishes

✉ **Tenzin Hotel, 8 Banjialing Lu** ☎ **(0892) 882 2018** 🕐 **Breakfast, lunch and dinner**

Turpan

John's Information Café (£)
Chinese and Western dishes and free travel information and advice. Internet access.

✉ **Opposite the Turpan Hotel** ☎ **(0995) 852 4297** 🕐 **Breakfast, lunch and dinner**

Urumqi
Try any of the small Muslim restaurants on Xinhua Lu or explore the night market on Changjiang Lu.

Fast Food
If you desperately need a break from Chinese cuisine, China has a growing list of fast-food restaurants that can be found even in some of the smaller cities. These include McDonald's, A&W, KFC, Popeye's, Baskin Robbins, Hagen Daz, Starbucks, Pizza Hut, Pizza Factory and many more. On the up-market side, TGIFs, Hardrock Café, Outback and Tony Romas can be found in Beijing and Shanghai.

Northern China

Prices

Prices are per room and per night excluding breakfast.

£ = under 500 yuan
££ = 500–1500 yuan
£££ = over 1500 yuan

Hotels

Like other countries, China rates its tourist hotels from one to five stars. That said, some Chinese hotels, with state connections, have the top five-star rating, while some better, less well-connected hotels may be a four or a three. Generally speaking, hotels with less than a four star rating will offer less comfortable accommodation, and poorer service, the lower the number, the more Spartan the accommodation. However, there are exceptions to this rule, and in fact, there are some quite good small hotels around the country that make up in good service and cleanliness what they lack in expensive trappings.

Beijing

Bamboo Garden Courtyard (Zhuyuan Binguan) (£)

Attractive mid-range courtyard hotel to the northwest of the Drum and Bell Towers.

✉ **24 Xiaoshiqiao Hutong, Jiugulou Dajie** ☎ **(010) 6403 2229; fax: (010) 6401 2633; www.bbgh.com.cn**

Beijing Hotel (£££)

Beijing's oldest hotel, and since its recent refurbishment still one of its best. A great location within walking distance of Tiananmen Square and the Forbidden City.

✉ **33 Dongchang'an Dajie, Dongcheng District** ☎ **(010) 6513 7766; fax: (010) 6513 7307; www.chinabeijinghotel.com**

Far East Hotel (£££)

Great value accommodation in a fine location in the middle of Beijing's *hutongs*. Also offers bike rental.

✉ **90 Tieshuxie Jie, Qianmenwai** ☎ **(010) 6301 8811, fax: 6301 8233**

Great Wall Sheraton (£££)

Located near Beijing's diplomatic area. The excellent facilities include health club, night-club, tennis courts, swimming pool and a series of fine restaurants.

✉ **10 Dongsanhuanbei Lu** ☎ **(010) 6500 5566; fax: (010) 6500 1938; www.sheratonbeijing.com**

Haoyuan Binguan (£)

Great value, low-key courtyard hotel hidden away in one of Beijing's famous *hutongs* to the east of Wangfujing.

✉ **53 Shijia Hutong** ☎ **(010) 6512 5557; (010) 6525 3179**

Lusongyuan Binguan (£)

A traditional walled courtyard hotel in Beijing's historic *hutong* area, originally built by a Mongolian general in the Qing dynasty.

✉ **22 Banchang Hutong, Kuan Jie, Dongcheng District** ☎ **(010) 6401 1116; fax: (010) 6403 0418**

Red Capital Residence (££)

A small boutique hotel (just five suites) located in a traditional courtyard house. Each of the five suites has an intriguing name such as 'The Chairman's Residence' or 'Concubine of the East'.

✉ **9, Dongsiliutiao** ☎ **(010) 6402 7150; e-mail: info@redcapitalclub.com.cn**

Shangri-La Hotel (£££)

Another one of China's superb string of Shangri-La hotels. Located in northwest Beijing this place has every conceivable facility, including its own delicatessen and shopping arcade. Well placed for the Summer Palace.

✉ **29 Zizhuyuan Lu, Haidian District** ☎ **(010) 6841 2211; fax: (010) 6841 8006; www.shangri-la.com**

St. Regis Hotel (£££)

A first-class hotel located on the grounds of the historic Beijing International Club and close to Beijing's Jian Guo Men Wai business district. Facilities include a spa and indoor heated pool.

✉ **21 Jianguomenwai Dajie** ☎ **(010) 6460 6688; fax: (010) 6460 3299; www.starwood.com**

Tiantan Haoyuan Hotel (££)

Beautifully located, stylish courtyard hotel, close to Tiantan Park. Maintains a charming sense of history.
B9A Tiantandong Lu ☎ (010) 6701 2404

Chengde

Mountain Villa Hotel (£)

Perfectly located for the Imperial Summer Palace. The hotel boasts six restaurants, a business centre and a variety of suites and rooms to suit all tastes
✉ 127 Xiaonanmen ☎ (0314) 202 5588; fax: (0314) 202 4143; www.hemvhotel.com

Datong

Yungang Binguan (£)

With a branch of CITS within the hotel this is a good place to book trips to the Hanging Temple. Rooms are comfortable with few facilities.
✉ 21 Yingbindong Lu ☎ (0352) 502 1601; fax: (0352) 2502 4927

Harbin

Holiday Inn (££)

Close to Harbin's historic Daoliqu area and St Sophia's Church. Facilities include a gym, sauna and massage rooms.
✉ 90 Jingwei Jie ☎ (0451) 422 6666; fax: (0451) 422 1661; e-mail: holiday@public.hr.hl.cn

Pingyao

Tianyuankui Minfeng Binguan (£)

Fabulously atmospheric Qing-era hotel, it used to house travelling merchants. Helpful staff make booking tickets very straightforward.
✉ 73 Mingqing Dajie ☎ (0354) 568 0069; fax: (0354) 568 3052; www.pytyk.com

Tianjin

Hyatt Hotel (Tianjin Kaiyue Fandian) (££)

Located in the centre of the city. Noted for its fine Xiang Wei Zhai Dumpling Restaurant. Other facilities include a riverside jogging circuit.
✉ 219 Jiefangbei Lu ☎ (022) 2330 1234; fax: (022) 2331 1234; www.tianjin.regency.hyatt.com

Wutaishan

Qixiange Binguan (£)

The best accommodation at the foot of the mountain. Peaceful setting close to nature.
✉ 2.5km south of Taihuai, near Nanshan Monastery ☎ (0350) 654 2400

Xi'an

City Hotel (Xi'an Chengshi Jiudian) (£)

This moderately priced hotel has clean rooms with helpful staff.
✉ 70 Nan Dajie ☎ (029) 721 9988; fax: (029) 721 6688

Hyatt Regency Xi'an (Xian Kaiyue Fandian) (£££)

Within the walls of the old city. The grand interior and the high standards of service make this hotel a delight. Amenities include a fitness club and indoor pool.
✉ 158 Dong Dajie ☎ (029) 769 1234; fax: (029) 769 6799; www.xian.regency.hyatt.com

Toilets

Toilets in public places and smaller restaurants and shops are usually the squat type, which are usually more sanitary than Western toilets, but difficult for some to use. It's best to make use of restrooms in hotels and fast-food restaurants. Make sure to always carry some toilet paper as many restrooms do not provide this amenity.

101

Eastern China

Courtyard Hotels
Traditional courtyard-style hotels – with their interesting architecture, quiet gardens and yards, and some interesting Chinese interior touches – offer a pleasant and inexpensive alternative to typical tourist hotels.

Hangzhou

Shangri-La Hotel (Xianggelila Fandian) (£££)

Beautifully located amid lush gardens and overlooking Hangzhou's famed West Lake. With a fitness centre, snooker and billiards hall, indoor swimming pool and sauna this is the best equipped hotel in town.

✉ 78 Beishan Lu ☎ (0571) 8797 7951; fax: (0571) 8707 3545; www.shangri-la.com

Huangshan

Beihai Binguan (£)

The best hotel for those wanting to catch the sunrise or sunset from the top of the mountain. It's a 20-minute walk away from the White Goose Peak cable car. Facilities are adequate.

✉ Beihai Scenic Area, eastern steps of the mountain ☎ (0559) 558 2555; fax: (0559) 558 2996

Luoyang

Peony Plaza Hotel (££)

Located at the heart of Luoyang, all rooms have satellite television and air-conditioning. Indoor swimming pool. The popular Manhattan Disco throbs to the beat nightly.

✉ 2 Nanchang Lu ☎ (0379) 493 1111; fax: (0379) 493 0303

Nanjing

Jinling Fandian (£££)

Just about the best hotel in town, located in the very heart of bustling Nanjing. Swimming pool, sauna and steam room, shopping arcade, and a number of excellent restaurants.

✉ 2 Hanzhong Lu, Xinjiekou Square ☎ (025) 471 1888; fax: (025) 471 1666; www.jinlinghotel.com

Qingdao

Shangri-La Hotel (£££)

In the east of the town, this typically plush and elegant member of the elite Shangri-la chain has an indoor pool, fitness centre, tennis courts and the famed Shang Palace Cantonese restaurant.

✉ 9 Xianggangzhong Lu ☎ (0532) 388 3838; fax: (0352) 388 6868; www.shangri-la.com

Qufu

Queli Binshe (£)

The best hotel in Qufu and right next to the famous Confucian Temple. The staff greet visitors with one of Confucius' famous quotes, 'It is wonderful to have friends from afar!' All rooms have satellite television and minibar.

✉ 1 Queli Jie ☎ (0537) 441 1300; fax: (0537) 441 2022

Putuoshan

Sanshengtang Fandian (£)

This used to be a huge monastery. Facilities are limited, but it's a good starting point for walks around the island.

✉ 121 Miaozhuangyan Lu ☎ (0580) 609 1277; fax: (0580) 609 1140

Shanghai

East Asia Hotel (£)

Situated on Shanghai's famous shopping street this old hotel provides a budget

alternative to the city's more expensive accommodation. Restaurants include Cantonese, Shanghai-style and French.

✉ 680 Nanjingdong Lu ☎ (021) 6322 3223; fax: (021) 6322 4598

Grand Hyatt Pudong (£££)

The Jinmao Tower is the third tallest building in the world and the Hyatt starts on the 53rd floor. The inner atrium stretches up to the tower's viewing level. The hotel boasts extensive spa facilities, indoor swimming pool, sauna and a weight room.

✉ Jinmao Building, 88 Shiji Dadao, Pudong ☎ (021) 5049 1234; fax: (021) 5049 1111; www.shanghai.grand.hyatt.com

Peace Hotel (£££)

Shanghai's classic old hotel situated right on the Bund. You get a real sense of history walking its corridors. Facilities are not as extensive as they should be for a hotel of this standing, but access to Nanjing Street and the Bund make up for this.

✉ 20 Nanjingdong Lu ☎ (021) 6321 6888; fax: (021) 6329 0300

The Portman Ritz-Carlton (£££)

Winner of numerous 'Best Hotel' awards this giant, 564-room hotel caters to all tastes. Health club, large shopping mall and 24-hour business centre. Also houses the renowned Summer Pavilion Chinese Restaurant.

✉ Shanghai Centre, 1376 Nanjingxi Lu ☎ (021) 6279 8888; fax: (021) 6279 8800; www.ritzcarlton.com

Sofitel Hyland Hotel (££)

Not far from the superb Shanghai Museum and a short walk from the Bund. Amenities include its own nightclub, sauna room and German Brauhaus.

✉ 505 Nanjingdong Lu ☎ (021) 6351 5888; fax: (021) 6351 4088; e-mail: sofitel@hyland-shanghai.com

Suzhou

Bamboo Grove Hotel (£££)

Well located for many of Suzhou's famous gardens. Comfortable and friendly hotel with gym, tennis courts, sauna and massage centre, and an extensive range of shops.

✉ 168 Zhuhui Lu ☎ (0512) 6520 5601; fax: (0512) 6520 8778; www.bamboo.sz.js.cn

Nanyuan Guest House (££)

Good value accommodation within a beautiful walled garden compound. The garden changes with the seasons and is stunning at all times. All rooms have satellite television and air-conditioning.

✉ 249 Shiquan Jie ☎ (0512) 6519 7661; fax: (0512) 6519 8806; e-mail: office@szny.com.cn

Wuxi

Holiday Inn Milido Wuxi (££)

Close to the centre of Wuxi. Comfortable and moderately priced with limited facilities. All rooms are equipped with satellite television and mini-bar.

✉ 2 Liangxi Lu ☎ (0510) 586 5665; fax: (0510) 580 1668

Tipping

Tipping is officially discouraged in China, but custom varies. While there are signs in some hotels advising guests not to tip staff, bellboys will expect a tip for carrying your bag to your room. Tipping is not standard in Chinese restaurants, as a service charge is added to the bill. However, tips may be expected in Western restaurants frequented by foreigners. Taxi drivers are never tipped unless they perform some extra assistance.

Southern China

Water

Water must be boiled before drinking and so you're advised not to drink tap water in your hotel room. Most hotels provide boiled or bottled water in the rooms. Water served in all hotels and restaurants is boiled, distilled or bottled mineral water. In more traditional hotels, you will find a Chinese hot water bottle placed in your room. Call room service for refills. In smaller hotels in out of the way places, hot water for bathing may only be available for a few hours in the early morning and evening.

Dali

Jim's Guesthouse (Heping Zhaodaisuo) (£)

The guesthouse's attached café, Jim's Peace Café, was one of Dali's first places to open for tourists after travel restrictions were lifted in 1985. Basic, comfortable rooms with 24-hour hot water. Still very popular with independent travellers.

✉ 63 Boai Lu, Dali Old Town ☎ (0872) 267 1822; fax: (0872) 267 0188

Jinhua Hotel (£)

Located at the very heart of ancient Dali. All rooms provide cable television and the hotel has a friendly bar and lounge.

✉ Corner of Huguo Lu and Fuxing Jie ☎ (0872) 267 3343; fax: (0872) 267 3846

Guangzhou

White Swan Hotel (Baitian'e Binguan) (£££)

With a perfect view of the Pearl River this is the best hotel in town. Superb facilities including two swimming pools, fitness centre, indoor and outdoor tennis courts and a number of fine restaurants.

✉ 1 Shamiannan Jie, Shamian Island ☎ (020) 8188 6968; fax: (020) 8186 1188; www.whiteswanhotel.com

Shamian Hotel (£)

Situated on the south of Guangzhou's Shamian Island, this is a good value budget option. Not too many amenities, but it does have a sauna room and swimming pool.

✉ 52 Shamiannan Jie ☎ (020) 8191 2288; fax: (020) 8191 1628

Guilin

Sheraton Guilin (££)

Well located on the Li River. Facilities include a health club and snooker room.

✉ Binjiangnan Lu ☎ (0773) 282 5588; fax: (0773) 282 5598

Hong Kong

Ritz-Carlton (£££)

Perfectly located at the heart of the Central District on Hong Kong Island. This is one of the best hotels in the world, small, but perfect. Choose between sweeping harbour views or breathtaking city vistas.

✉ 3 Connaught Road, Central ☎ (852) 2877 6666; fax: (852) 2877 6778; www.ritz-carlton.com

Kowloon Hotel (££)

Part of the Peninsula group, an advantage if you stay here as you can use the nearby Peninsula Hotel's facilities. Situated in the centre of Hong Kong's best shopping area.

✉ 19–21 Nathan Road, Tsim Sha Tsui ☎ (852) 2929 2888; (852) 2739 9811; www.fasttrack.kowloon.penins ula.com

Macau

Pousada de Sao Tiago (£££)

Beautifully located at the tip of the Macau Peninsula with a superb view over the Pearl River Delta. With 23 rooms the hotel is built into the site of a Portuguese fort.

✉ Avenida de Republica, Fortaleza de Sao Tiago da Barra ☎ (0853) 378-111; fax: 552-170

Northwest China

Chengdu

Holiday Inn Crowne Plaza Chengdu (£££)

The top hotel in Chengdu and situated in the heart of the city. Great restaurants and fitness facilities, and the popular Rainbow Crowne Nite Club is booming every night.

✉ 31 Zhongfu Lu ☎ (028) 8678 6666; fax: (028) 8678 9789; e-mail: cpchengdu@eichuan.net.cn

Chongqing

Wudu Binguan (££)

A standard, moderately priced hotel with a pretty good French restaurant.

✉ 24 Shang Zhengjiayan, Zhongshansi Lu, Yuzhongqu ☎ (023) 6385 1788; fax: (023) 6385 0762

Chongqing Shipin Mansion (£)

Excellent value budget accommodation, all rooms are air-conditioned and they sell tickets for cruises on the Yangzi River.

✉ 72 Shaanxi Lu ☎ (023) 6384 7300; fax: (023) 6384 5844

Dazu

Dazu Hotel (£)

Best location for visiting Beishan and Baodingshan. Amenities include a fitness centre and a night club.

✉ 47 Gongnong, Longgang Town ☎ (023) 4372 1888

Dunhuang

Silk Road Dunhuang Hotel (Dunhuang Shanzhuang) (££)

Incredible location in the sand dunes south of town. The hotel provides every possible convenience including camel riding, sand sledding and archery.

✉ Dunyue Lu ☎ (0937) 888 2088; fax: (0937) 888 2086; www.the-silk-road.com

Emeishan

Hongzhushan Hotel (£)

With its close proximity to the mountain this is probably the best place to stay in Emeishan.

✉ Near the Baoguo Monastery ☎ (0833) 522 5888; fax: (0833) 552 5666

Kashgar

Qianhai Hotel (£)

A quiet, laid back place with a few facilities including a couple of quite reasonable restaurants.

✉ 199 Renminxi Lu ☎ (0998) 282 2922; (0998) 282 0644

Lhasa

Lhasa Hotel (££)

Comfortable three-star hotel with five restaurants and satellite television in every room. This place has hot water all year round, something that cannot be said for some of Lhasa's other hotels.

B1 Minzu Lu ☎ (0891) 683 2221; fax: (0891) 683 5796

Turpan

Oasis Hotel (Luzhou Binguan) (£)

Another hotel in the Silk Road chain. Facilities include an Internet café and sauna room. The Muslim restaurant serves excellent regional specialities.

✉ 41 Qingnianbei Lu ☎ (0995) 852 2491; fax: (0995) 852 3348; www.the-silk-road.com

Room Keys

In many smaller Chinese hotels you will not be given a room key. In these establishments, there will be a room attendant on each floor who will be the only one who can open your door for you. This can sometimes be a bit inconvenient when the person cannot be immediately found.

Shopping in China

Antiques

Antiques, artwork, and other items that are considered cultural relics cannot be taken out of the country without proper certification. If you're planning to take your purchase back home, you must have your item marked with a red wax seal before heading for the airport. This can be done at the Friendship Store on Jianguomenwai Dajie. Customs officials will seize any item deemed to be a cultural relic that does not have the proper certification.

Arts and Crafts

Beijing

Beijing Curio City (Beijing Guwen Cheng)

With more than 200 stalls to choose from, the choice of antiques is immense. Some genuinely old, others perhaps just created last week.

✉ 21 Dongsanhuannan Lu, Chongwen District ☎ (010) 6774 7711 to 63

Beijing Yihong Carpet Factory

The showrooms here are filled with old carpets and rugs from Mongolia, Tibet and Xinjiang.

✉ 35 Juzhang Hutong, Fahuasi Jie, Chongwen District (near the Hongqiao Market) ☎ (010) 6712 2195

The Friendship Store

A wide collection of items, from embroidered tablecloths to carpets, antiques, silk clothing, jewellery, cloisonné, porcelain, etc. This is not the cheapest (or most expensive) place to shop for such items, but it is state run and reliable.

✉ 17 Jianguomenwai Dajie ☎ (010) 6500 3311

Gangchen Carpets

Beautiful and authentic Tibetan carpets made in Tibet with excellent highland sheep wool.

✉ 1/F, Kempinski Hotel ☎ (010) 6465 3388 ext. 5542

Hongqiao Market

Also known as the Pearl Market, in addition to fresh water pearls and other jewellery, Hongqiao also sells a wide variety of handicrafts and name brand copies.

✉ 16 Hong Qiao Lu (across from the east gate of the Temple of Heaven), Chongwen District ☎ (010) 6711 7429, 6711 7499

Liulichang

A row of curio and book shops in a remodelled Qing Dynasty street.

✉ One block south and east of the Xuanwumen subway station

Panjiayuan Folk Culture Market

An amazing collection of items sold in an open-air market: everything from genuine antiques to fakes (beware): handicrafts, paintings, porcelain, religious art, minority crafts, etc. Open Saturdays and Sundays from around sunrise. Come in the morning.

✉ Just west (inside) the east third ring road, between Panjiayuan Bridge and Huawei Bridge ☎ (010) 6775 2405

Qianmen Carpet Factory

A wide variety of carpets from Tibet and Xinjiang as well as silk carpets from Henan can be purchased, also expert restoration.

✉ 44 Xingfu Dajie, Chongwen District ☎ (010) 6715 1687

Ruifuxiang Silk and Cloth Store

Raw silk, a wide array of colours, textures and patterns, is the main attraction here. In business for more than a century and used to serve Qing royalty.

✉ 5 Dazhanlan Jie, Xuanwu District

Hong Kong

Amazing Grace Elephant Company

A multitude of arts and crafts from all over East Asia. A great place to find unusual gifts.

✉ **349 Ocean Centre, Harbour City, Kowloon** ☎ **(852) 2730 5455**

Eastern Dreams

Reproduction furniture, screens, ceramics and woodcarvings. They specialise in Ming and Qing period pieces.

✉ **47A Hollywood Road, Central** ☎ **(852) 2544 2804**

Shanghai

Arts and Crafts Institute

Home to a number of workshops where craftsmen turn out everything from bamboo and sandalwood carvings to inlaid lacquer ware and embroidery.

✉ **79 Fenyang Lu** ☎ **(021) 6437 2509**

Friendship Store

A large selection of interesting, although expensive, antiques, porcelain and cloisonné are available at this state-run shop.

✉ **40 Beijingdong Lu** ☎ **(021) 6329 7374**

Friendship Store, Antiques Branch

Specialising in antiques. Good quality cloisonné also available.

✉ **694 Nanjingxi Lu** ☎ **(021) 6253 8092**

Fuyou Market

Shanghai's most famous antiques market, open Sundays just outside the Old Town. Bargaining is a must.

✉ **Fangbangzhong Lu**

Gu Yue Xuan

An interesting assortment of old clocks and watches at negotiable prices. Other oddities include beautiful old painted snuff bottles.

✉ **378 Changle Lu** ☎ **(021) 6218 3316**

Jiya

A respected antiques dealer with an extensive assortment of collectables.

✉ **899 Huqingping Highway** ☎ **(021) 6479 1051**

Shanghai Jingdezhen Porcelain Artware Shop

A large collection of quality porcelain items.

✉ **1175 Nanjingxi Lu** ☎ **(021) 6437 2509**

Zhumin Ming & Qing Furniture Shop

Not just furniture: a variety of small collectables at reasonable prices.

✉ **299 Henannan Lu, Nanshi District** ☎ **(021) 6328 8491**

Tianjin

Ancient Culture Street

Scrolls, seals, ceramics and other Chinese crafts.

✉ **Guwenhua Jie (at the corner of Dongma Lu and Beima Lu)**

Shenyangdao Antique Market

Everything from antiques to jade, scrolls, porcelain and Mao memorabilia

✉ **Corner of Jinzhou Dao and Shandong Lu**

Caveat Emptor

Chinese 'antique' markets are piled high with fake items, some carefully inlaid with a coating of dust to make them look like they're fresh from the excavation site. Unless you're an expert, one is advised to beware before snapping up that beautiful Ming vase.

Silk

The production of silk was invented in China, and the country is today the number one producer of this product. Chinese markets sell a wide variety of quality, inexpensive silk items – blouses, underwear, scarves, ties, jackets, robes, bedspreads, sheets, and pyjamas – that make great gifts for friends back home.

Art Galleries

Beijing

Courtyard Gallery

Paintings and sculptures by well-known contemporary Chinese artists in a modern courtyard house beside the moat of the Forbidden City. Western restaurant on the first floor.

✉ 95 Donghuamen Dajie (next to the east gate of the Forbidden City) ☎ (010) 6526 8882

Redgate Gallery

Contemporary Chinese art displayed in one of the few remaining gates of the old Beijing city wall

✉ The Watchtower (Dongbianmen, corner of the Second Ring Road) ☎ (010) 6525 1005

Shanghai

Shanghai Museum Shop

A large collection of tasteful art reproductions, paintings, stationary, books and more. Well worth visiting if you're in the museum.

✉ 201 Renmin Lu ☎ (021) 6372 3500

Books and Music

Beijing

Wangfujing Xinhua Bookstore

Plenty of English-language books, maps and postcards.

✉ 235 Wangfujing Dajie (beside Oriental Plaza) ☎ (010) 6512 6922

Hong Kong

Page One

Huge English-language bookshop, the best in Hong Kong. Plenty of fiction and non-fiction.

✉ Times Square, 1 Matheson Street, Causeway Bay ☎ (852) 2506 0383

Shanghai

Shanghai Foreign Languages Bookstore

All kinds of foreign language books, primarily English, but some in Spanish, French, German and other languages, as well as CDs and videos.

✉ 390 Fuzhou Lu ☎ (021) 6322 3200

Shops, Malls and Department Stores

Beijing

China World Shopping Mall

Large, all purpose shopping complex. It reckons it's 'the number one shopping address in China'. Plenty of beautiful textile shops and a fine selection of antique stores.

✉ 1 Jianguomenwai Dajie, Chaoyang District ☎ (010) 6505 2288

Lufthansa Centre

Great range of goods, including cosmetics, electronics and a Western-style supermarket on the ground floor.

✉ 52 Liangmaqiao, Chaoyang District ☎ (010) 6465 1188

Oriental Plaza

Beijing's biggest shopping mall.

✉ Wangfujing ☎ (010) 8518 8888

Silk Alley (Xiushui Jie Shichang)

A large collection of name brand copies and factory seconds – check your purchase carefully for defects. Silk Alley also carries inexpensive silk items and handicrafts. Be prepared to bargain.

⊠ Jianguomenwai, 50m west of Dongdaqiao Lu, Chaoyang District

Hong Kong

Harbour City

A megamall, one of the world's largest. Located right next to the Star Ferry, it stretches for many blocks up Canton Road. Every conceivable name in world retailing can be found within its walls.

⊠ Canton Road, Tsim Sha Tsui
☎ (852) 2118 8668

Pacific Place

With more than 200 stores and restaurants this is the largest shopping complex on Hong Kong Island. Marks & Spencer, Body Shop, Cartier, Hermès and virtually every other designer name.

⊠ 88 Queensway, Central
☎ (852) 2801 4197

Shanghai

Isetan

Japanese-run department store selling international, Japanese and local products.

⊠ 537 Huaihaizhong Lu
☎ (021) 5306 1111

Shanghai No. 1 Department Store

Recently renovated this old pre-liberation stalwart has a wide range of international and Chinese products.

⊠ 830 Nanjingdong Lu ☎ (021) 6322 3344

Shopping Streets

Beijing

Qianmen Dajie and Dazhalan

This has long been famous as a shopping mecca. The small streets that cut across this area are crowded with small shops, many selling traditional items, such as silk and cloth. You will also find some interesting examples of turn-of-the-century European architecture in this old section of town.

Wangfujing Dajie

Although this old street, once Beijing's premier shopping area, has been recently renovated, with much of it taken up by new upscale shopping malls, it still has a large selection of interesting small and old shops. The first few blocks have now been closed to most traffic, and so this is a great place for a stroll and some window-shopping.

Xidan

This bustling street to the west of Tiananmen Square, is where the younger generation shops for inexpensive clothes. A good place to rub elbows with Chinese.

Shanghai

Nanjing Dong Lu

Shanghai's premier shopping street, packed with small shops, boutiques and large department stores. Today this largely pedestrianised commercial centre is the heart of modern Shanghai.

Bargaining

Bargaining is usually not common in department stores, hotels or up-market shops, but is a part of the game in indoor and outdoor markets and stalls and small shops catering to tourists. Bargaining is part of the fun of shopping in China, so remember to be polite and keep smiling. Sellers usually double the price of a good, and so experienced buyers will start with less than half the price asked; sellers will sometimes inflate the price by several times. Never let the seller realise how much you want a product; you may even want to feign a bit of disinterest. A common technique is to walk away if the seller refuses to budge on the price. If he or she is willing to accept your price, you won't get far from the stall before they come after you. If not, you can always shop around, and go back later and pay the best price offered. It is also advisable to walk through the market asking different sellers what their prices are for the items you want to buy before making your purchase – you'll sometimes find a seller offering the same item at a hugely lower price. Above all, be patient and remember to give the seller some face.

Children's China

Acrobatics
The art of acrobatics dates back more than 4,000 years in China, and it's still a popular folk art. Special schools enrol primary school children to begin the rigorous training to become an acrobat. Acrobats are also an important part of traditional opera performances, such as Beijing Opera and the old school of opera known as Kunqu.

Beijing

Beijing Amusement Park
A traditional amusement park with ferris wheels, roundabouts, boat rides, roller-coaster, and a waterslide for the warmer weather.

✉ **Longtan Park, Chongwen District** ☎ (010) 6701 1155 ⏰ 8:30–5:30 🚌 60 💷 **Expensive**

Beijing Aquarium
Located next to the Beijing zoo and features a fine selection of marine life. Highlights include a killer whale show and a shark tank.

✉ **137 Xizhimenwai Dajie, Xicheng District** ☎ (010) 6217 6655 ⏰ 9–5:30 🚇 Xizhimen 🚌 7, 15, 102, 103, 111, 332 💷 **Expensive**

Beijing Chaoyang Theatre
The China Acrobatic Troupe offers a nightly performance of the very highest standard. Their repertoire includes tightrope walking, plate spinning, juggling, and mindboggling gymnastic displays.

✉ **36 Dongsanhuanbei Lu, Chaoyang District** ☎ (010) 6507 2421 ⏰ Daily 7:15pm 💷 **Moderate**

Beijing Zoo
Not the most inspiring zoo in the world, but it is worth a visit for the giant pandas.

✉ **137 Xizhimenwai Dajie, Xicheng District** ☎ (010) 6831 4411 🚇 Xizhimen 🚌 7, 15, 102, 103, 111, 332 💷 Cheap

Bird Park
A reasonably large selection of colourful birds.

✉ **18 Beituchengxi Lu, Chaoyang District** ☎ (010) 6237 9927 ⏰ 8:30–5 💷 Cheap

Blue Zoo Beijing
Underwater aquarium with an electric moving walkway. Thousands of fish living in as natural environment as possible.

✉ **Worker's Stadium (South Gate), Chaoyang District** ☎ (010) 6591 3397 ⏰ 9–8 💷 **Moderate**

Daoxianghu Riders' Riding Club (Daoxianghu Machang)
For horse riding this park is one of the better places in Beijing. They have experienced instructors and it's also a good area to while away a few hours.

✉ **Inside Daoxianghu Park, Sujiatuo Village** ☎ (010) 6245 5879 💷 **Moderate**

Fandoule (Fun Dazzle)
For children between about 3 and 10. Large play area with slides and 'jungle' style gym equipment.

✉ **Worker's Stadium, near South Gate, Chaoyang District** ☎ (010) 6593 6193 💷 Cheap

Lakeview Waterpark
A huge water amusement park with a beach that's possible to surf, waterslides, tubing and a vortex pool for adults.

✉ **2 Fuqian Street, near Yanqi Lake, Huairou County** ☎ (010) 6562 8838 💷 **Expensive**

Le Cool
Large ice skating rink.

✉ **B2, China World, 1 Jianguomenwai Dajie** ☎ (010) 6505 5776 ⏰ 10–10 💷 Cheap

Hong Kong

Ocean Park

A vast complex including an amusement park, cable-car ride, oceanarium, and the Middle Kingdom theme park.
✉ **Wong Chuk Hang Road, Hong Kong Island** ☎ **(852) 2552 0291** 🕐 **Daily 10–6**
💷 **Expensive**

Science Museum

A host of interactive displays that ought to keep the kids engaged for hours.
✉ **2 Science Museum Road, Tsim Sha Tsui, Kowloon** ☎ **(852) 2732 3232** 🕐 **Mon, Tue, Wed, Fri 1–9, Sat, Sun 10–9. Closed Thu** 💷 **Expensive**

Shanghai

Fun Dazzle

Large indoor playground with a variety of padded slides and jungle gym equipment for children ages around 3 to 8.
✉ **780 Changning Lu, in Zhongshan Park** ☎ **(021) 6210 7388** 💷 **Cheap**

Science and Technology Museum

Interactive museum split into five main themes including Earth Exploration, Children's Technoland, Light of Wisdom, Spectrum of Life, and Cradle of Designers.
✉ **2000 Shijidadao, Century Park, Pudong** ☎ **(021) 6862 2000** 🕐 **Tue–Sun 9–5:30** 🚇 **Yanggao Nanlu** 💷 **Expensive**

Shanghai Acrobatics Theatre

A daily hour-and-a-half show with breathtaking feats of strength and skill.
✉ **1376 Nanjingxi Lu** ☎ **(021) 6279 8663** 💷 **Moderate**

Shanghai Botanical Gardens

With several children's playgrounds the gardens are a good place to enjoy a few relaxing hours. Divided into sectors specialising in ferns, bamboo, magnolias and many other plant and flower species.
✉ **1111 Longwu Lu, south of Longhua Lu, Xuhui District** ☎ **(021) 6451 3369** 🕐 **8–4** 💷 **Cheap**

Shanghai Circus World

China has always been renowned for its circuses. Groups from all over the world come here to perform in this huge domed structure.
✉ **2266 Gonghexin Lu, near Daning Lu** ☎ **(021) 6652 7750**

Shanghai Wild Animal Park

Home to more than ten thousand animals this drive-through safari is well worth the 35km trip from downtown Shanghai. Children can feed the monkeys and various other animals.
✉ **Nanhuisan Zao Zhen, Pudong** ☎ **(021) 5803 6000** 🕐 **8–5** 💷 **Moderate**

Shanghai Zoo

One of China's better zoos. Unusual and rare animals include the South China tiger, Siberian tiger, red goral, ring-tailed lemur and oriental white stork. Other facilities include a roller-skating rink, and children's playground.
✉ **2381 Hongqiao Lu (near the old airport)** ☎ **(021) 6268 7775 ext, 3098** 🕐 **9–4:30** 🚌 **57** 💷 **Cheap**

Children

Chinese people love kids, and are curious about Western children, especially those with blond hair and blue eyes. If you have small children travelling with you in China, expect to have people on the street, trains and restaurants make a fuss over them. You will undoubtedly also have many requests from strangers to take a photo with your little ones. Remember that this is a good-natured interest – take a minute for a group photo and you'll see some smiling Chinese faces.

The Arts

Cinema

While films made in China after 1949 were all propagandistic, contemporary Chinese directors have won acclaim in the West, snapping up a number of prestigious international awards. Unfortunately, many of these films are banned in China, while those that are available in the country are all on VCD, and few have English subtitles. You can, however, buy DVD and video versions of these films overseas. Some of the more popular modern Chinese films include: *King of Masks*; *The Black Cannon Incident*; *Ju Dou*; *My Father, My Mother*; *Hang the Red Lantern*; *Not One Less*; *Blue Kite*; *Red Sorghum*; *Keep Cool*; *Yellow Earth*; *Er Mo*; *The Old Well*; *The Story of Jiuqu*, *Hero* and *Farewell My Concubine*.

Beijing

Cherry Lane Cinema

This non-profit service was established to provide foreign viewers with exposure to the best of contemporary Chinese films. Chinese movies with English subtitles are shown Friday and Saturday evenings at 8PM. Directors and actors are sometimes on hand for a discussion with the audience. Check *City Weekend* for titles, dates and times. Or visit www.cherrylanemovies.com .cn

✉ **Sino-Japanese Youth Centre, 40 Liangmaqiao Lu** ☎ (010) 6461 5318

Grand View Garden Theatre

Peking opera and banquet. Operas used to last many hours, but here it is cut to a more manageable two hours maximum.

✉ **12 Nancaiyuan Jie, Xuanwu District** ☎ (010) 6351 9025 ⏰ Daily 7:30PM

Laoshe Teahouse

Featuring opera, magic tricks and acrobatics. The opera shows are usually enlivened with comedy routines (don't worry if you can't understand Chinese, these passages are highly visual).

✉ **3 Qianmenxi Dajie, Chongwen District** ☎ (010) 6303 6830 ⏰ Daily 7:40 and 9:20PM

Liyuan Theatre

This has now become Beijing's leading opera house. Screens alongside the stage show English translations and this certainly helps you appreciate what is going on.

✉ **Qianmen Hotel, 175 Yongan Lu, Xuanwu District** ☎ (010) 6301 6688 ext. 8860 ⏰ Daily 7:30PM

Sanwei Bookstore

Traditional Chinese music performed by some of Beijing's best classical musicians in a rustic teashop. Reservations recommended.

✉ **60 Fuxingmennei Dajie** ☎ (010) 6601 3204 ⏰ Sat 8:30–10:30PM

Zhongguo Mu'ou Juyuan

The ancient art of Chinese shadow and hand puppetry is kept alive here at the China Puppet Art Theatre. Troupes from all over China regularly visit the theatre. Performances only at weekends.

✉ **1 Anhuaxili, Chaoyang District** ☎ (010) 6424 3698 ⏰ Sat 10:30AM and 3PM; Sun 3PM

Hong Kong

Hong Kong Academy for Performing Arts

With two large theatres the academy sees regular international dance performances as well as pop and rock concerts.

✉ **1 Gloucester Road, Wan Chai** ☎ (852) 2584 8500

Hong Kong Cultural Centre

The Cultural Centre comprises a 1,750-seat Grand Theatre and a 2,100-seat hall and is the home of the Hong Kong Philharmonic Orchestra – one of the best orchestras in the world. Other regular events include drama productions and

movie screenings.

✉ 10 Salisbury Road, Tsim Sha Tsui ☎ (852) 2734 9009

Hong Kong Fringe Club

Plays host to a variety of alternative performers. Jazz, theatre, poetry, classical music, also an important venue for Hong Kong's annual City Festival.

✉ 2 Lower Albert Road, Central ☎ (852) 2521 7251

Lijiang

Naxi Orchestra

A 24-piece orchestra playing on traditional Naxi instruments. Kublai Khan is supposed to have been the original patron of this ancient musical tradition. The Cultural Revolution saw many instruments destroyed, fortunately these musicians managed to hide their own.

✉ Naxi Music Academy, Dong Dajie ⏰ Daily 8–10PM

Shanghai

Dashijie (Great World)

Acrobatics, magic shows, folk dancing, films and art exhibitions. Also a variety of regional Chinese opera styles including Suzhou, Yangzhou and Ningpo.

✉ 1 Xizhangnan Lu ☎ (021) 6326 3760 ext. 40 or 57

Shanghai Concert Hall

This is the home of the Shanghai Symphony Orchestra. Check local listings magazines for performances.

✉ 523 Yan'andong Lu ☎ (021) 6437 7504

Shanghai Drama Arts Centre

A small theatre with consistently good productions. It's managed to attract such well-known groups as the Royal Shakespeare Company who performed here in 2002.

✉ 201 Anfu Lu ☎ (021) 6433 5133

Shanghai Grand Theatre

A huge, superbly designed modern opera house with a spectacular curved roof. The building contains three separate theatres, each welcoming artists from all over the world.

✉ 300 Renmindadao ☎ (021) 6372 8701

Studio City

Large, modern movie hall with six screens showing all the latest blockbusters from around the world. Soundtracks in Chinese and English.

✉ 10/F Westgate Mall, 1038 Nanjingxi Lu ☎ (021) 6218 2173

Yifu Theatre

A famous old Beijing Opera theatre where the greatest stars of this traditional art have all performed.

✉ 701 Fuzhou Lu ☎ (021) 6351 4668

Suzhou

Garden of the Master of the Nets

Nightly hour-long performances including traditional local opera, dance and theatre performances. The audience moves around the gardens.

✉ Shiquan Jie ☎ (0512) 6520 3514 ⏰ Daily 7:30–9:30PM

Beijing Opera

Also known as Peking Opera, this is an old form of theatre combining acting, singing, dancing, martial arts and acrobatics accompanied by loud traditional music. Actors wear colourful clothes and their faces are painted in bright colours that represent the role they're playing. The stories come from traditional plays and novels. Elderly Chinese can often be seen in parks singing their favourite passages from well-known operas, accompanied by a musician playing the erhu, a traditional Chinese instrument.

Nightlife

Nightlife

Major cities such as Beijing and Shanghai are experiencing a rapid growth in entertainment facilities, from theme restaurants to uniquely designed bars and coffee shops. Check out the weekly English entertainment guides and websites (➤ 116) for the latest news of what to do. In smaller, out-of-the-way areas karaoke may be the main form of entertainment, but unfortunately, the quality of these establishments is often quite poor, and some are quite seedy and even dishonest. Unless you're with Chinese friends, it might be better to avoid nightlife in these places.

Beijing

Big Easy

Cajun and Creole cuisine accompanied by live jazz and blues every evening in this elegant Louisiana-style restaurant.

✉ **East side of the south gate, Chao Yang Park, Chaoyang District** ☎ **(010) 6508 6776**
🕐 **Daily 5PM–2AM**

CD Café

Live music performed by local and foreign jazz and rock groups. Beijing's top venue for live rock.

✉ **Dongsanhuan Lu, south of the Agricultural Exhibition Centre** ☎ **(010) 6501 8877 ext 3032** 🕐 **Daily 8–2:30**

Jazz Ya

This Japanese-style bar and restaurant is one of the oldest in Beijing. It has long been a favourite with the expat crowd who come here to enjoy Jazz Ya's extensive collection of jazz recordings.

✉ **Sanlitun North Bar Street, located in an alley opposite the China Commercial Bank**
☎ **(010) 6415 1227**

Neo Lounge

This upscale bar, restaurant and dance club, is a popular hangout for Beijing's trendy crowd.

✉ **99 Xinfucunzhong Lu**
☎ **(010) 6416 1077**

Suzie Wong

A tastefully decorated bar furnished with traditional Chinese furniture.

✉ **West gate of Chaoyang Park**
☎ **(010) 6593 6049**

The Loft

Early evening this stylish restaurant, bar and disco serves great French cuisine, then from around 11pm onwards the music gets cranked up. Thought to be the coolest nightspot in Beijing.

✉ **4 Gongtibei Lu, west of the Zhaolong Hotel, Chaoyang District** ☎ **(010) 6501 7501**
🕐 **Daily 11AM–2AM**

Shanghai

Hard Han Café Theatre

Restaurant cum café, cum theatre cum disco.

✉ **555 Zhaojiabang Lu, Xu Jia District** ☎ **(021) 6443 5935**

Old China Hand Reading Room

Bar, café and library all rolled into one. An excellent selection of books on old Shanghai and other subjects. The Old China Hand is decorated with interesting art and antiques, making it a great place to relax with a drink.

✉ **27 Shaoxing Lu** ☎ **(021) 6473 2526**

O'Malley's Irish Pub

This cosy bar, located in an old Shanghai mansion, has an elegant hardwood interior and authentic Irish antiques. An ideal place for enjoying a drink outdoors in the warm weather.

✉ **42 Taojiang Lu** ☎ **(021) 6474 4533**

Peace Hotel

1940s jazz performed every evening in the lobby of the old Peace Hotel.

✉ **Peace Hotel, 20 Nanjingdong Lu** ☎ **(021) 6321 6888**

Sports

Beijing

Beijing International Club

Indoor and outdoor tennis courts.

✉ 21 Jianguomenwai Dajie, Chaoyang District ☎ (010) 6532 2046

Beijing International Golf Club (Ming Tombs Golf Course)

About one hour from the centre of Beijing, this is the capital's best course.

✉ North of Shisanling Reservoir, Changping County ☎ (010) 6974 5678, 6974 6388

Capital Gymnasium

Badminton, table-tennis, basketball and a climbing centre.

✉ 54 Baishiqiao Lu, Haidian District ☎ (010) 6833 5552
🕐 Daily 9AM–10PM

China World Hotel Health and Fitness

Squash courts, indoor tennis courts, swimming pool.

✉ 1 Jianguomenwai Dajie, Chaoyang District ☎ (010) 6505 2266 🕐 Daily 6AM–10PM

Huatang International Golf Club

Championship standard 18-hole course and Beijing's newest links.

✉ Sanhe Yanjiao Development Zone ☎ (010) 6959 1771

Lido Club

Health club with a well-equipped gym and also squash courts, tennis, steam bath and sauna.

✉ Jichang Lu, Chaoyang District ☎ (010) 6437 6688
🕐 Daily 6:30AM–11PM

Movenpick Hotel Splash Club

Health facilities and sporting possibilities include horse riding and snooker.

✉ Xiao Tianzhu Village, Shunyi County ☎ (010) 6456 5588 ext 1217 🕐 Daily 6–11

Shidu Bungee Jumping Facility

The first bungee jump in China, with high and low jumps.

✉ 88km southwest of Beijing, Fangshan District, Du You Lan Area ☎ (010) 6134 0084
🕐 Daily 8–6

Yuanmingyuan Paintball Field

Best place for paintball action.

✉ The Old Summer Palace, East of Fuhai Lake ☎ (010) 6257 6598

Shanghai

Disc Kart Indoor Karting

Over 4,500sq m indoor go-kart racing track.

✉ 326 Aomen Lu ☎ (021) 6277 5641 🕐 Daily 2PM–2AM

IB Racing Kart Club

Outdoor leisure and racing go-karts.

✉ 880 Zhongshanbeiyi Lu, Hongkou District ☎ (021) 6531 6800 🕐 Daily 10–6 (later in summer)

Masterhand Rock Climbing Club

Indoor and outdoor rock climbing, hiking, mountaineering and camping.

✉ No. 21 Upper Stand, 444 Dongjiangwan Lu ☎ (021) 5696 6657 🕐 Daily 10–10

Sports

Chinese are avid sports fans and there are a growing number of sports venues and activities springing up around the country, from rock climbing, to bungee jumping, basketball, volleyball and badminton. Go to any public park in the morning, and ask to participate in the *taiqi* or martial arts, or cut up the pavement with the ballroom and disco dancers. There are amateur running clubs in major cities, as well as hiking, mountain climbing and biking clubs. Check the source listings (➤116) for up-to-date details.

What's on When

Event Listings
For up-to-date information on where to eat, shop and play in major cities check out City Weekend, the bi-weekly English newspapers, *That's Beijing*, *That's Shanghai* and the monthly *That's Guangzhou* are available in leading hotels and restaurants. Also check out their frequently updated websites at www.cityweekend.com.cn and www.thatsbeijing.com, which has a wide range of information. Also on the Internet is www.xianzai.com, offering weekly listings of events.

The dates of traditional Chinese holidays and festivals vary from year to year according to the lunar calendar.

January/February
Chinese Lunar New Year: the most important holiday of the year for the Chinese begins on the first day of the lunar calendar's first moon. Families come together to enjoy special meals and to light fireworks. Lively temple fairs are held in major parks during this holiday. Many shops and restaurants close for several days during this time.

Lantern Festival: this popular celebration, marking the end of the Spring Festival, falls on the 15th day of the first lunar month. People buy paper lanterns – illuminated by candles or battery-powered light bulbs – and walk through parks and streets.

The Tibetan Lunar New Year, which falls in January or February, is marked by archery and horseback competition, religious dances and other ceremonies.

Guanyin's Birthday: marks the birthday of Guanyin, the Goddess of Mercy, on the 19th day of the second moon.

April
Qingming (Tomb Sweeping) Festival: traditional holiday when Chinese tidy up the burial places of their ancestors.

Water Sprinkling Festival of the Dai nationality.

May
May Day: International Labour Day is now celebrated in China as a week-long holiday. This is not a good time to travel in China, as transportation and hotels can be difficult to book in some areas of the country (1 May).

May/June
Dragon Boat Festival: commemorates the death of Qu Yuan, a patriot and poet who drowned himself as an act of political protest. This day is marked by dragon boat races and the consumption of zongzi, bamboo leaves stuffed with sticky rice and other fillings, such as meat, peanuts, or red bean paste.

June
Children's Day (1 June): teachers, parents and children go to parks and on field trips

August/September
The Autumn Moon Festival (15th day of the 8th moon) celebrates a 14th century uprising against the Mongols. People present friends with Moon cakes, prepared with a variety of fillings.

October
National Day (1 October) commemorates the founding of the People's Republic of China. In some years large military parades are staged in front of the Gate of Heavenly Peace. The government has designated this as a week-long holiday. Hotel room availability and transportation can be difficult during this time.

POLICE 110

FIRE 119

AMBULANCE 120

TOURIST HOTLINE (010) 6513 0828

WHEN YOU ARE THERE

ARRIVING

Most tourists arrive at Beijing International Airport or Shanghai Pudong International Airport. Travel by train is possible from Mongolia, Russia, Vietnam and Hong Kong.

Beijing Int. Airport
Kilometres to city centre

25 kilometres

	Journey times
	N/A
	1 hour
	40 minutes

Shanghai Pudong Airport
Kilometres to city centre

30 kilometres

	Journey times
	25 minutes
	50 minutes
	40 minutes

MONEY

The monetary unit of China is the renminbi (RMB), also known as the yuan. It is divided into 10 jiao and further subdivided into 10 fen. Yuan and fen are also colloquially known as kuai and mao. The Bank of China issues RMB notes in denominations of 1, 2, 5, 10, 20, 50 and 100 yuan. Jiao and fen are of so little value that visitors need not be concerned with these denominations. Major credit cards are accepted in all large cities and most airports and city banks have facilities for changing foreign currency and travellers' cheques.

Outside large cities credit cards may not be accepted everywhere and cash is more dependable. Cash may be obtained from Bank of China ATM machines in major cities with most international ATM cards.

TIME

China is 8 hours ahead of Greenwich Mean Time (GMT+8). The whole country lies within the same time zone. Daylight saving time is not used.

CUSTOMS

YES

There are specific allowances for the import of alcohol, cigarettes and luxury goods into the country for those over 18 years of age:

Alcohol: 2 litres
Cigarettes: 400
Perfume: 0.5 litres
Gold: 50 grams
There are no restrictions on currency importation, but not more than RMBY6,000 may be exported.
When departing be careful that any antiques you have purchased are permitted to leave the country. You may not export antiques. Antiques that are permitted for export must bear a red seal, obtainable in Beijing at the Friendship Store, and any item not carrying the seal may be seized at customs. Hold on to your receipts in case customs officers request them.

NO

Non-prescription drugs, pornography, firearms, certain fruits and vegetables.

UK	Germany	USA	Netherlands	Spain
☎ (010) 6532 1961	☎ (010) 6532 2161	☎ (010) 6532 3831	☎ (010) 6532 1131	☎ (010) 6532 1986

WHEN YOU ARE THERE

TOURIST OFFICES

Beijing
Beijing Tourism Group
Ground Floor
Beijing Tourist Building
28 Jianguomenwai Dajie
☎ (010) 6515 8562

China Youth Travel Service
(CYTS)
23C Dongjiaomin Xiangnei
Dongcheng District

Hong Kong
China International Travel
Service (CITS)
New Mandarin Plaza, Tower
A, 12th Floor
14 Science Museum Road
Tsimshatsui East
Kowloon
☎ (852) 2732 5888

Shanghai
China International Travel
Service (CITS)
1st Floor
Guangming Building
2 Jinlingdong Lu
☎ (021) 6321 7200

NATIONAL HOLIDAYS

J	F	M	A	M	J	J	A	S	O	N	D
6	5	1		2	1	1	1		1		

China's official national holidays are:

1 Jan	New Year's Day
Jan/Feb	Chinese New Year (5 days)*
8 March	International Women's Day
1 May	International Labour Day
4 May	Youth Day
1 June	International Children's Day
1 July	Birthday of the Chinese Communist Party
1 August	People's Liberation Army Day
1 Oct	National Day

*Governed by the lunar calendar

OPENING HOURS

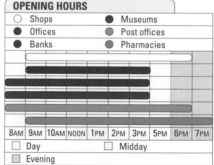

○ Shops	● Museums
● Offices	● Post offices
● Banks	● Pharmacies

| 8AM | 9AM | 10AM | NOON | 1PM | 2PM | 3PM | 5PM | 6PM | 7PM |

□ Day   □ Midday
□ Evening

Some banks open on Saturdays between 8 and 11:30.
In the larger cities some pharmacies stay open 24
hours. Small shops are usually open by 8am and tend
to close by 6pm. Department stores open around
10am and close as late as 10pm. Museums are often
closed on Mondays. Markets open as early as 3am
and many are finished by 8am, others stay open until
the early afternoon. All government offices, post
offices and banks close for national holidays.

DRIVE ON THE
RIGHT

TOILETS
POOR

NO STARS

PUBLIC TRANSPORT

Internal Flights There is a comprehensive domestic air network. Planes are generally more expensive than trains. Major carriers are Air China, China Northern, China Northwest, China Eastern, and China Southern. Some provincial governments also run their own airlines.

Trains China's rail network is excellent and is the country's main means of transportation. There are soft sleeper berth (four people sharing one cabin), hard sleeper berth (six people sharing a section in an open car), soft seats and hard seats.
Beijing Railway Hotline ☎ (010) 6563 3662

Buses They are widely used within and between towns and cities, although the quality and comfort varies sharply, and generally speaking is not good. Bus tours arranged by China International Travel Service are generally reliable. Buses are generally viewed as less safe as highway conditions are poor in some areas, and because traffic can be chaotic on highways around the country

Ferries There are ferry services from Hong Kong to Guangzhou and Shanghai. The trip to Guangzhou takes about 12 hours on the overnight ship, or four hours on jetfoils. The trip to Shanghai takes three days. There is also a ferry service along the Yangzi River, and between cities on the east coast, such as Dalian – Yantai and Shanghai – Ningpo. You can also take a tourist boat along the Grand Canal, from Hangzhou to Suzhou.

CAR RENTAL

Renting your own car is possible in Beijing, Hong Kong, Macau and Shanghai, but at the moment you are only allowed to drive within the city's boundaries. It is better to hire your own driver, especially for trips outside the city to scenic spots. It's faster and inexpensive.

TAXIS

Taxis are cheap and convenient Few drivers speak English, so it's advisable to have your destination written in Chinese, and to always carry a business card from your hotel with its address in Chinese. city. Patronise only taxis from the line in front of the main doors of the airport terminal.

DRIVING

Speed limits on expressways:
120kph

Speed limits on main roads:
90kph

Speed limits on urban roads:
90kph

It is compulsory for drivers and passengers to wear seat belts on highways.

Random breath testing is not common in China, but drunken driving and other traffic offences are dealt with severely. Police are strict and ready to issue traffic tickets.

Fuel is available as leaded and unleaded petrol and as diesel, and is sold by the litre. It is served by attendants. Credit cards are not accepted. Cash only.

There are no organisations in China that provide road assistance. However, the explosive growth of automobile ownership may support a service in the near future.

PERSONAL SAFETY

China is relatively safe, and although theft is rare, you are advised to take usual precautions. Pickpockets are common on crowded city streets and on buses, so place your passport and wallet in a safe place. In restaurants, train and bus stations and other public places keep a close watch on your bags and other valuables. There is a lot of counterfeit money floating around China, so do not change currency with money exchangers on the street.

Police assistance:
☎ **110** from any call box

TELEPHONES

Public telephones are hard to find sometimes. Calls cost 50 fen for a local call. IP cards can be purchased at newspaper booths for long-distance calls. The rate is less expensive than the Beijing Telecommunications Company.

POST

Post Offices
Open 8–6 Mon–Sun (no packages can be sent on either Sat or Sun). The airmail rate for postcards is 4.20 yuan. Letters 5.40 yuan to Europe, USA and Canada. Letters 2.00 yuan to Hong Kong and Southeast Asia.

ELECTRICITY

China's power supply is 220 volts. Beijing plugs come in a variety of sizes. Although most hotels can provide adapters, if you are travelling with mobile phones, laptop computers, or other items that need to be plugged in it is advisable to carry adapters with you.

TIPS/GRATUITIES

Yes ✓ No ✗		
Restaurants	✗	
Tour Guides	✓	5–10%
Taxis	✗	
Porters	✓	5–10%
Chambermaids	✗	
Hairdressers	✗	
Toilets	✗	

Tipping is officially discouraged in China, but tour guides and staff at hotels who carry bags will often expect a small tip.

PHOTOGRAPHY
What to photograph: mountains, gardens, temples, old courtyards, city gates, snow scenes in winter, blossoms in spring and autumn.
Restrictions: photography is forbidden in many museums and archaeological sites (most notably the Terracotta Warriors).
Where to buy film: department stores and kiosks at sightseeing spots. Kodak has a nation-wide chain of photography outlets.

HEALTH

Insurance
All visitors are strongly recommended to arrange medical insurance before leaving for China; this should include transport home. Medical facilities are good.

Dental Services
Most tourist hotels should be able to recommend a good dental clinic. Any treatment will need to be paid for and then reclaimed on insurance.

Sun Advice
Central and southern China can be hot and sticky, while the north is extremely dry. It is easy to become dehydrated so it is essential to drink plenty of water. Always ensure that children are properly protected.

Drugs
Bring a good supply of prescription drugs in case they are difficult to find. Chinese pharmacies sell much of the same range of everyday medicines you would find in Western Europe or America. There are English-speaking pharmacists at some clinics in the larger cities, but prices for medicine at foreign clinics can be steep. Hotel shops usually carry basic over-the-counter drugs.

Safe Water
Tap water in China is not safe to drink, unless so specified in hotel rooms, and so must be boiled before drinking. Water served in hotels and restaurants has been boiled and so is safe to drink. Bottled water is widely available at restaurants, small shops and kiosks. It is not advisable to walk barefoot in rice paddies or other wet areas.

CONCESSIONS

Students/Youths Discounts on entry to tourist sites are only offered to foreign students enrolled at local universities and upon presentation of a valid student ID. In China few concessions are made to youth.

Senior citizens A few tourist attractions offer discounts to senior citizens (bring some identification). Otherwise there are almost no concessions for the older traveller, this however is more than made up for by the way in which the Chinese treat older people. Age implies status and respect.

CLOTHING SIZES

CHINA	USA	UK	Europe		
36	36	36	46		
38	38	38	48		
40	40	40	50		Suits
42	42	42	52		
44	44	44	54		
46	46	46	56		
7	8	7	41		
7.5	8.5	7.5	42		
8.5	9.5	8.5	43		Shoes
9.5	10.5	9.5	44		
10.5	11.5	10.5	45		
11	12	11	46		
14	14.5	14.5	37		
15	15	15	38		
15.5	15.5	15.5	39/40		Shirts
16	16	16	41		
16.5	16.5	16.5	42		
17	17	17	43		
8	6	8	34		
10	8	10	36		
12	10	12	38		Dresses
14	12	14	40		
16	14	16	42		
18	16	18	44		
4.5	6	4.5	37.5		
5	6.5	5	38		
5.5	7	5.5	38.5		Shoes
6	7.5	6	39		
6.5	8	6.5	40		
7	8.5	7	41		

WHEN DEPARTING

- There is a 90 yuan airport tax payable on leaving China; a 50 yuan airport tax is charged for domestic flights.
- Make sure that you reconfirm your onward flight no fewer than 72 hours before departure.
- Arrive at the airport two hours before departure time for international flights, one hour for domestic flights.

LANGUAGE

On the whole few Chinese speak much English, although most young people and students are very enthusiastic to speak to you. Knowledge of a few words might be useful and helpful.

Chinese characters are rendered into the Latin alphabet by the official system of Romanisation known as pinyin. It is largely pronounced as written, but note the following:

a as in car; c as in bits when an initial consonant; e as in her; i as in feet unless preceded by c, ch, r, s, sh, z, sh, when it becomes er as in her; j as in gin; o as in ford; q like the ch in chin; s as in simple; u as in oo in cool; w as in wade, though pronounced by some as v, x like the sh in sheep but with the s given greater emphasis; y as in yoyo; z as ds in lids; zh as j in jam.

hotel	*fan dian*	how much is it?	*duo shao qian?*
guest house	*bing guan*	room	*fang jian*
do you have a room?	*ni you bu you fang jian?*	bathroom	*xishou jian*
		toilet	*ce suo*

how much is this?	*zhei shi duo shao qian?*	6	*liu*
too expensive	*tai gui*	7	*qi*
inexpensive	*bu gui / pian yi*	8	*ba*
0	*ling*	9	*jiu*
1	*yi*	10	*shi*
2	*er*	11	*shiyi*
3	*san*	20	*ershi*
4	*si*	30	*sanshi*
5	*wu*	100	*yibai*
		1,000	*yiquian*

rice	*fan*	pork	*zhu rou*
noodles	*mian tiao*	shrimp	*xia*
fried rice	*chao fan*	soup	*tang*
egg	*ji dan*	fruit	*guo zi*
fish	*yu*	boiled water	*kai shui*
duck	*ya*	tea	*cha*
chicken	*ji*	coffee	*ka fei*
beef	*niu rou*	beer	*pi jiu*

aeroplane	*fei ji*	taxi	*chu zu qi che*
airport	*fei ji chang*	bicycle	*zi xing che*
bus	*gong gong qi che*	I would like to go...	*wo yao qu*
bus station	*gong gong qi che zhan*	Where is the...?	*...zai nar?*
train	*huo che*	I would like a ticket	*wo yao mai piao*
railway station	*huo che zhan*		

hello	*ni hao?*	I don't understand	*wo bu dong*
goodbye	*zai jian*		
How are you?	*ni hao ma?*	Do you understand?	*ni dong bu dong?*
Well, thank you.	*hen hao, xie xie*		
thank you	*xie xie ni*	yes	*shi*
When?	*shen me shi hou?*	no	*bu shi*
		I like...	*wo xihuan*
It doesn't matter	*mei you went ti*	I don't like...	*wo bu xihuan*
What is this?	*zhei shi shen mo?*	today	*jin tian*
		yesterday	*ming tian*
I understand	*wo dong*	tomorrow	*zuo tian*

INDEX

Acknowledgements

The Automobile Association wishes to thank the following photographers, libraries and associations for their assistance in the preparation of this book:

CPA MEDIA LIBRARY 14b, 16, 19; **JIM GOODMAN/CPA** 7c, 13c, 20, 21c, 21b, 24, 25c, 71, 78; **OLIVER HARGREAVE/CPA** 10c, 11; **DAVID HENLEY/CPA** 1; 2, 5a, 5b, 6, 7b, 8, 9c, 9b, 10b, 13b, 14c, 15a, 15b, 18, 22b, 25b, 27a, 27b, 30, 37, 40, 44, 45, 48, 50, 51, 52, 54, 55, 56, 57, 58a, 58b, 59a, 59b, 60a, 60b, 61, 62, 64, 65, 66, 67, 68, 69, 70, 74, 75, 76, 77a, 79, 84, 85, 87, 91a, 91b, 117a, 117b, 122a, 122b; **ZHANG XUEZHONG/CPA** 12, 80, 81, 89, 90; **RON EMMONS** 86; **E. J. HAAS** 43, 49, 88; **TERRY MADISON/MADISON IMAGES** 17, 26, 31, 32, 36, 38, 39, 41, 42, 77b; **PAUL MOONEY** 33, 46, 47

AA PHOTO LIBRARY 22c, 23

The remaining pictures are from the Association's own library **(AA WORLD TRAVEL LIBRARY)** and were taken by: **G Clements** F/Cover (b) child, (c) performer, (d) Temple of Quinian Hall, (e) national flag and B/Cover; **A Kouprianoff** F/Cover (a) lion, Beijing, (g) person in yellow robe; **I Morejohn** F/Cover (f) Confucius statue, F/C bottom dragon bricks, Beijing.

Contributors
Copy Editor: Andrew Forbes / CPA Media

Page layout and cartography: Doug Gordon Morton / CPA Media, Chiang Mai,

Dear Essential Traveller

**Your comments, opinions and recommendations are very
important to us. So please help us to improve our travel
guides by taking a few minutes to complete this simple
questionnaire.**

*You do not need a stamp (unless posted outside the UK). If you do not want to cut this page
from your guide, then photocopy it or write your answers on a plain sheet of paper.*

Send to: **The Editor, AA World Travel Guides,
FREEPOST SCE 4598, Basingstoke RG21 4GY.**

Your recommendations...

We always encourage readers' recommendations for restaurants, nightlife
or shopping – if your recommendation is used in the next edition of the
guide, we will send you a *FREE* AA *Essential* **Guide** of your choice.
Please state below the establishment name, location and your reasons
for recommending it.

_____

_____

_____

_____

Please send me **AA *Essential*** _____
(*see list of titles inside the front cover*)

About this guide...

Which title did you buy?
  AA *Essential* _____
Where did you buy it? _____
When? __ __ / __ __

Why did you choose an AA *Essential* Guide? _____

_____

_____

_____

_____

Did this guide meet your expectations?
  Exceeded ☐ Met all ☐ Met most ☐ Fell below ☐
  Please give your reasons_____

_____

_____

_____

continued on next page...

Were there any aspects of this guide that you particularly liked? _____

_____

_____

_____

Is there anything we could have done better? _____

_____

_____

_____

_____

About you...

Name (*Mr/Mrs/Ms*) _____

Address _____

_____

_____ Postcode _____

Daytime tel nos _____

Which age group are you in?
Under 25 ☐ 25–34 ☐ 35–44 ☐ 45–54 ☐ 55–64 ☐ 65+ ☐

How many trips do you make a year?
Less than one ☐ One ☐ Two ☐ Three or more ☐

Are you an AA member? Yes ☐ No ☐

About your trip...

When did you book? m m / y y   When did you travel? m m / y y

How long did you stay? _____

Was it for business or leisure? _____

Did you buy any other travel guides for your trip?

If yes, which ones? _____

_____

Thank you for taking the time to complete this questionnaire. Please send
it to us as soon as possible, and remember, you do not need a stamp
(*unless posted outside the UK*).

Happy Holidays!

We may use information we hold to write or telephone you about other products and services
offered by us and our carefully selected partners. Information may be disclosed to other companies
in the Centrica group (including those using the British Gas, Scottish Gas, goldfish, One-Tel and
AA brands) but we can assure you that we will not disclose it to third parties. Please tick the
box if you do not wish to receive details of other products and services from the AA. ☐